MASTERS
OF THE
OCEAN REALM

Whales, Dolphins, and Porpoises

MASTERS OF TH

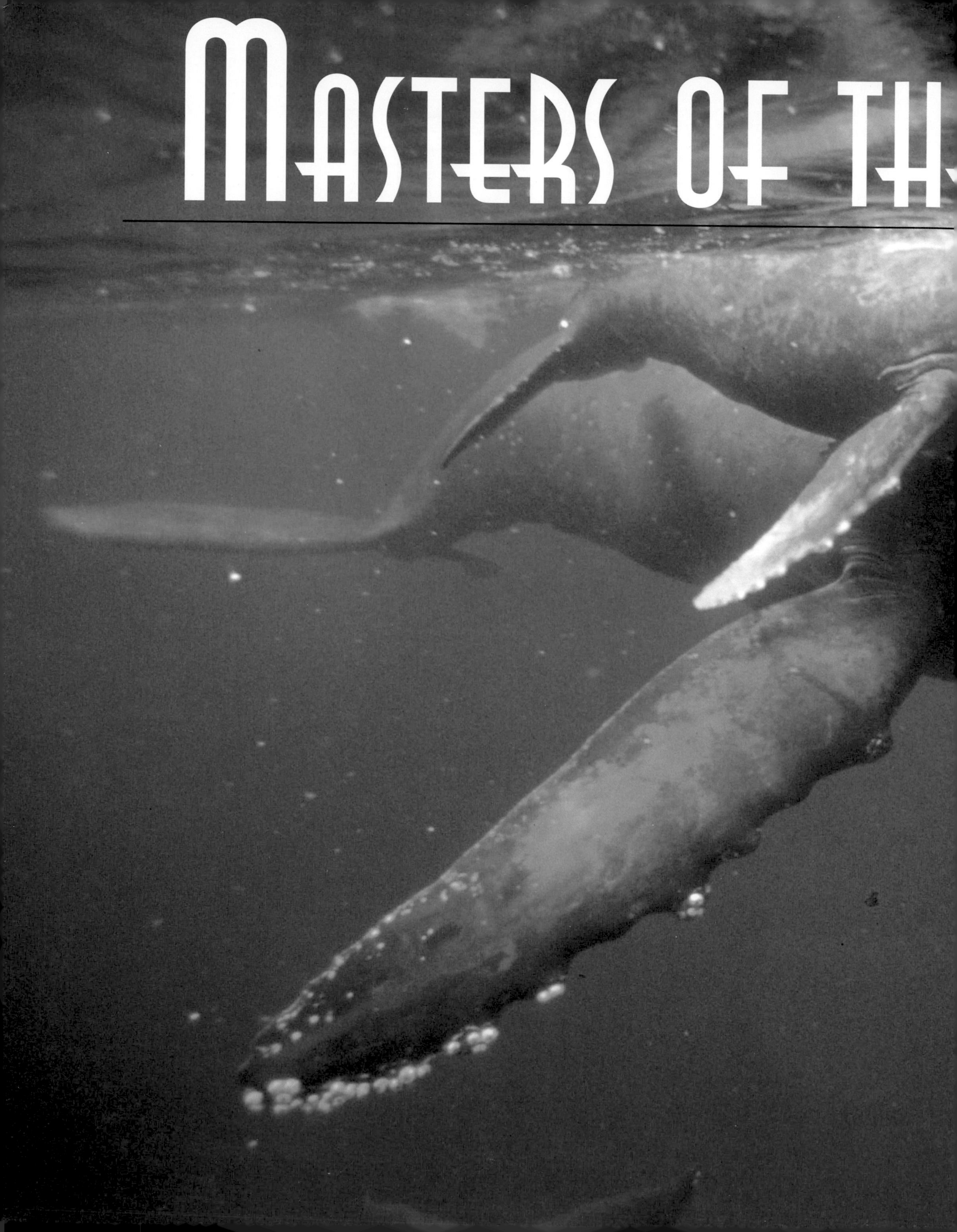

OCEAN REALM

Whales, Dolphins, and Porpoises

by John E. Heyning

University of Washington Press
Seattle & London
in association with the
Natural History Museum of Los Angeles County

Dedicated to Marlene Ann

Acknowledgments: I thank Cyrena Nouzille, designer of the exhibition for the Natural History Museum of Los Angeles County, who assisted in photograph and graphics selection and drafted many of the illustrations. Dr. Daniel M. Cohen, Dr. Kirk Fitzhugh, Kimball Garrett, Joan C. Grasty, Corinne Heyning, Cyrena Nouzille, Dr. Randall Wells, and Rosita Worl reviewed all or parts of the manuscript. Cheryl Braunstein assisted with early drafts of Chapter VI. Natural History Museum photographers Dick Meier, Dan Watson, and Justin De Leon supplied a number of the photographs in this book; museum model makers Steve Melendrez, Carol Ryan, and Caryl Castleberry created models for the exhibition. Materials referred to by LACM numbers are in the collections of the Natural History Museum of Los Angeles County.

Masters of the Ocean Realm: Whales, Dolphins, and Porpoises
is published in conjunction with the traveling exhibition of the same name, organized by the Natural History Museum of Los Angeles County.

Copyright © 1995 by the Los Angeles County Museum
of Natural History Foundation
Printed in Hong Kong by Midas Printing Company.

Published by the University of Washington Press, P.O. Box 50096, Seattle, WA 98145-5096.

Published simultaneously in Canada by UBC Press, University of British Columbia.

Library of Congress Cataloging-in-Publication Data

Heyning, John E. (John Edward)
    Masters of the ocean realm : whales, dolphins, and porpoises / John E. Heyning.
        p.   cm.
    Includes bibliographical references (p.   ) and index.
    ISBN 0-295-97487-7 (alk. paper)
    1. Cetacea. 2. Wildlife conservation. 3. Cetacea–Folklore.
    I. Title.
    QL737.C4H43 1995
    599.5—dc20   CIP 95-37435

The paper used in this publication meets the minimum requirements
of American National Standard for Information Sciences—Permanence of
Paper for Printed Library Materials, ANSI Z39.48-1984.

COVER: Atlantic spotted dolphins. BOB TALBOT

BACK COVER: Killer whales. © 1994 SEA WORLD OF CALIFORNIA, INC.

PAGE 1: A blue whale surfaces in the Sea of Cortez. With 2,000 animals, the Mexico-California population of blue whales may be the largest in the world. JOHN E. HEYNING.

TITLE PAGES: A humpback whale with her newborn calf. BOB TALBOT.

CONTENTS

INTRODUCTION

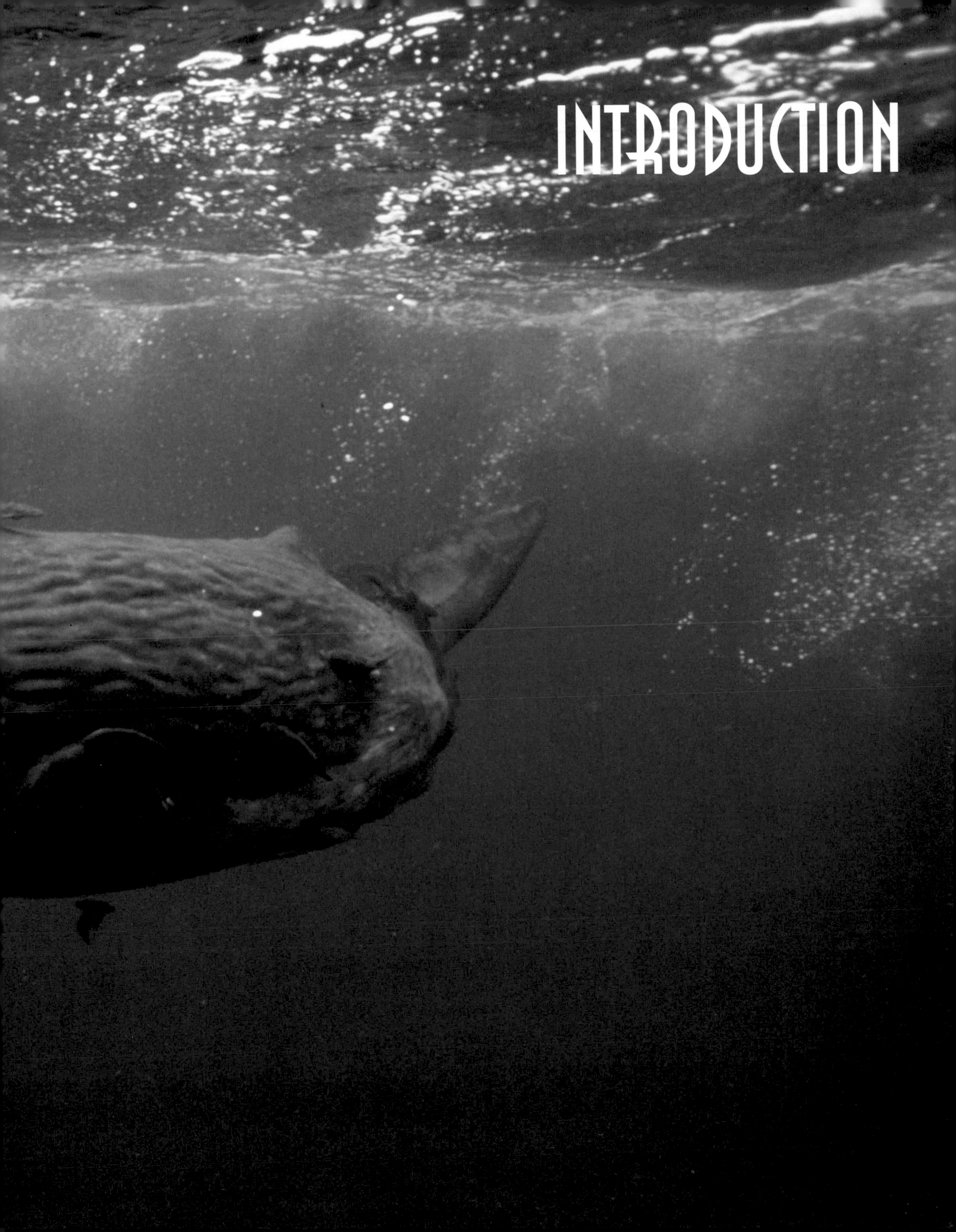

From the earliest times, people have encountered whales and dolphins and told stories about them full of questions and wonder. The Greeks told of dolphins that came to shore to play with children. The Bible describes a leviathan that swallowed Jonah to teach him a lesson from God. Arab cultures believed the entire world was supported by an angel standing on the back of a whale. In ancient and modern times, dolphins, whales, and people seem to have had a special connection.

For thousands of years, people have wondered about the origins of these marine mammals and their mysterious lives. The Greeks had one explanation. According to myth, Dionysus, the god of wine and revelry, once took passage on a ship. The sailors, however, were pirates and planned to enslave their passenger. When Dionysus discovered their plot, he avenged himself. As punishment, he caused the ship's mast to sprout branches, the men's oars to become snakes, and a strange flute to play. The terrified pirates threw themselves into the sea, where they were changed into dolphins and commanded to serve humankind.

Through careful observation and scientific research, we now know much about the dolphin and the whale and, as the legend suggests, we know we are closely linked—we are both air-breathing mammals. Whales, dolphins, and porpoises lead lives like our own, lives much more complex than we have suspected. They live in all the world's oceans, many seas, and even some rivers. As a group, they include the largest animal known to have existed on the planet, one of the most powerful hunters of modern times, and some of the most intelligent animals in the world.

Like distant cousins, whales, dol-phins, and porpoises are all related to each other. There are at least 79 **species**, or kinds, classified together in one group of marine mammals that scientists call **cetaceans**, from the Greek word *cetus*, meaning "whale."

To best understand how whales and dolphins live under water, imagine spending a day with them. You must surface for air, then hold your breath to swim and dive. You must stay warm, dive deep to catch your food, and not be crushed by the tremendous pressure of deep water weighing down on you. Your babies must be born under water, and you must protect yourself from sharks— all with no hands for grabbing, no clothes to keep you warm, no boats to rest in, and no trees to hide behind.

To stay under water for any length of time, a person needs special equipment—a tank of air, a rubber suit for warmth, and flippers for paddling about. Yet whales, dolphins, and porpoises live out their entire lives in the aquatic environment. By exploring the differences between humans and marine mammals, we can appreciate how cetaceans have adapted so well to their vast world and why they look more like fish than mammals.

Come meet these masters of the ocean realm, the whales, dolphins, and porpoises, and explore their lives— how they breathe, dive, give birth, and play, entirely in the water, an environment that people can only visit for a short time.

PAGES 6–7:
A sperm whale, the largest of the toothed whales, with remora fish on its back and sides. HOWARD HALL/ HOWARD HALL PRODUCTIONS.

OPPOSITE:
Atlantic spotted dolphins. BOB TALBOT.

BELOW:
The Dionysus Cup, illustrating an ancient Greek legend about the origin of dolphins. STAATLICHE ANTIKEN- SAMMLUNGEN UND GLYPTOTECK, MUNICH.

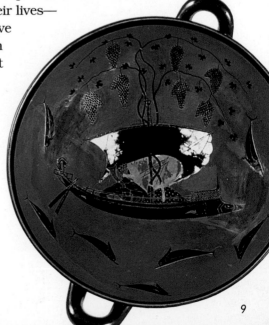

THE BASIC WHALE AND DOLPHIN

The condensing water vapor in this humpback whale's breath forms a spout or blow. BOB TALBOT.

To grow quickly and develop a thick layer of blubber for warmth, cetacean calves drink milk that is extremely high in fat. Human milk is about 1.5 percent fat, and cow's milk is about 4 percent fat. But cetacean milk is about 40 percent fat! On this rich drink, a blue whale calf gains about 175 pounds (80 kilograms) a day.

Nursing in the ocean poses some challenges. It is not easy to drink under water, and cetacean mothers often nurse their calves while swimming. To overcome such difficulties, cetaceans have evolved special muscles around the mammary glands that squirt milk quickly into the calf's mouth, which has a special tongue designed not to spill!

Most mammals give birth to live young rather than laying eggs, and cetaceans must all give birth to their young in the water. A baby cetacean usually slips out of the birth canal tail first instead of head first. And while most baby mammals slowly learn to make their way around, a newborn cetacean must swim immediately to the surface to take its first breath.

Like all mammals, cetaceans have lungs and so must come to the surface to breathe (fish and other aquatic animals take in oxygen directly from the water). The nostrils, or nose openings, of a cetacean are located on top of its head and are called the **blowhole**. When a whale or dolphin surfaces (comes to the surface to breathe), the blowhole opens quickly, first to exhale, then to inhale, filling the lungs with fresh air.

If you have ever seen a whale, you have probably first seen a whale spout. When larger dolphins and whales exhale, the water vapor in their breath makes a cloud, just as your own breath does on a cold day. The massive plume of water vapor from the enormous lungs of a whale is called the **spout** or **blow**. Whalers and experienced whale watchers can identify the species of whale from far away by the shape of its blow.

Whales breathe at the surface only a few times before they dive. Some cetaceans must surface again to breathe every few minutes, but other species, such as the sperm and bottlenose whales, can hold their breath for over an hour!

Because they are mammals adapted to the sea, cetaceans have characteristics not seen in land mammals. In fact, a cetacean looks more like a fish than a mammal. Its streamlined body allows it to swim easily through the water, which is also the reason that submarines and torpedoes are designed with this same shape. As part of this streamlined shape, cetaceans have no outer ears nor hind limbs, and their genitals and mammary glands are tucked within their bodies. Whales and dolphins also have shortened necks, and most fast-swimming, open-ocean cetaceans have little or no ability to move their necks. Species that live in shallow water have some neck movement so they can maneuver in tight places.

As streamlined as they are, cetaceans have almost all the bones that other mammals have. Their skeletons have no leg or foot bones but include arm bones and shoulder blades, ribs, backbones, and even the remnant of hip bones. Although some of these bones do not look or work exactly as they do in people, their positions within the cetacean's body are similar to the positions of our bones.

The fish-like streamlined body of a cetacean is an example of **convergent evolution**—where distantly related animals

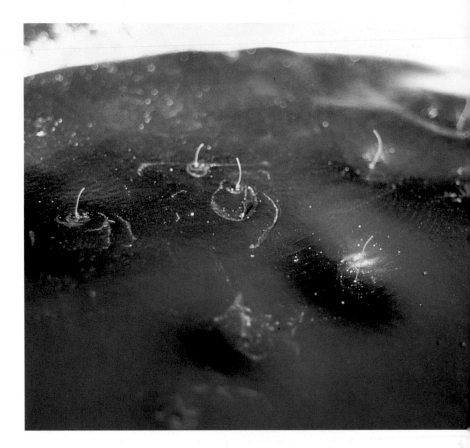

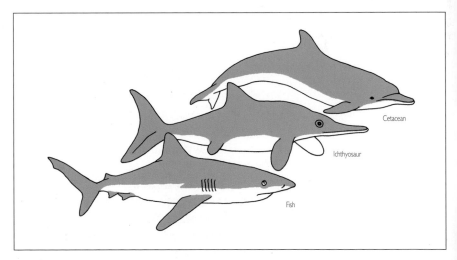

TOP:

Snout hairs on a newborn gray whale. Through evolution, whales and dolphins have lost nearly all their hair. LACM 88980; DICK MEIER.

BOTTOM:

The shark, the extinct marine reptile ichthyosaur, and the dolphin have each evolved a streamlined shape for moving quickly through water—an example of convergent evolution. CYRENA NOUZILLE.

evolve similar traits. The body shapes of cetaceans and fish are so similar that for centuries people thought cetaceans were fish! This streamlined body form evolved because it allowed both types of animals to move more successfully in their aquatic environment and thus better survive.

Most fish and most cetaceans have a fin along the top of their bodies. This **dorsal fin** evolved separately to give them stability as they swam. When we take a close look, we see that the whale's fin is very different from the fish's fin. The dorsal fin of a cetacean is made of connective tissue, like your ear lobes or the end of your nose. The dorsal fin of a fish is made up of many fine bones connected by a web of skin.

In cetaceans, the front legs have evolved into paddle-like **flippers**, which must be strong and stiff to steer and brake. No dolphin or whale could steer with flimsy flippers. How do cetaceans move their rigid flippers to steer? They use their shoulders to rotate their flippers just as we use our shoulders to move our arms.

The bones of the flipper are similar to the bones of the human arm and the bones of the front leg in other mammals; they include a shoulder blade (scapula), an upper arm bone (humerus), two lower arm bones (radius and ulna), wrist bones (carpals and metacarpals), and finger bones (phalanges). The "arm" bones of the cetacean are much shorter than those of a person of the same size, and its "fingers," hidden within the flipper, are much longer. Although the flipper of a cetacean, the arm of a human, and the front leg of a dog do not look alike and do not function in the same way, they are **homologous structures**—body parts that evolved from the same limb or organ of an ancient ancestor.

The broad tail of a cetacean is called

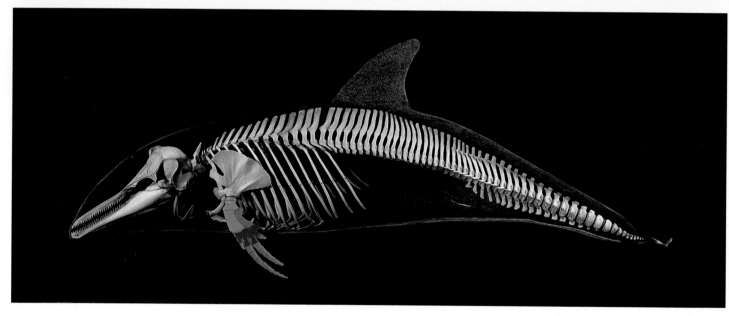

A model of a Pacific white-sided dolphin, showing external features and skeleton. Not surprisingly, some parts of a cetacean skeleton are different from those of other mammals. For example, the arm bones are shorter, the finger bones form the paddlelike flipper, and the hind legs have entirely disappeared. NATURAL HISTORY MUSEUM OF LOS ANGELES COUNTY MODEL; SKELETON LACM 31325; DICK MEIER.

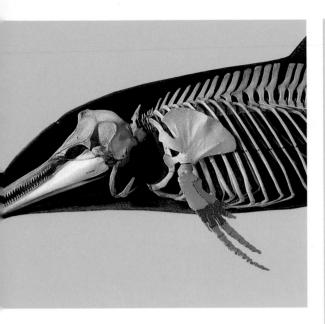

ED MASTRO

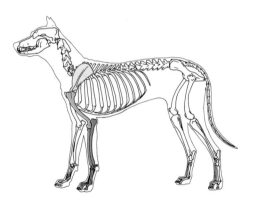

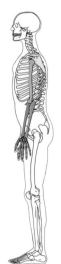

A person's arm, a dog's front leg, and a dolphin's flipper are all made of the same kinds of bones, yet they look different, and each performs a different function (grasping, walking, or steering). The three limbs are homologous structures. DETAIL OF SKELETON SHOWN ON PAGE 18; DRAWINGS BY CYRENA NOUZILLE.

The Hostess with the Mostest: Parasites

It is true that almost all wild animals have parasites, and whales and dolphins are no exception. Parasites are organisms that live on and feed on other organisms. Cetaceans may have parasites on the inside of their bodies as well as on the surface of their skin. Barnacles, a type of external parasite, are easy to see on many whales and on some dolphins. Barnacles are most abundant on slow-swimming gray and humpback whales. One humpback whale was reported to have been carrying over 1,000 pounds (450 kilograms) of barnacles!

Many species of whales and a few dolphin species also have whale lice, which are crustaceans related to sand fleas. The lice live in the folds and creases along a whale's body or between the barnacles.

When a whale breaches, it may be trying to shake off the pests. While some lice may be shaken off, barnacles dig into the whale's skin almost $1/2$ inch (1 centimeter), and not even a big breach can shake them loose.

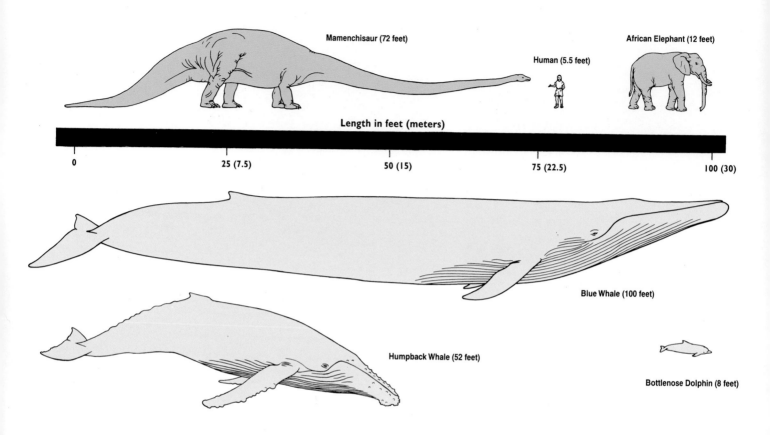

Length in feet (meters)

Mamenchisaur (72 feet)

Human (5.5 feet)

African Elephant (12 feet)

| 0 | 25 (7.5) | 50 (15) | 75 (22.5) | 100 (30) |

Blue Whale (100 feet)

Humpback Whale (52 feet)

Bottlenose Dolphin (8 feet)

The longest blue whales measure 100 feet (30 meters) in length and are the largest animals that have ever lived. CYRENA NOUZILLE.

the **flukes**. Both cetaceans and fish use their tails to swim, but the tail of a fish is vertical and moves from side to side. Cetaceans, however, have horizontal tails that move up and down. Although the cetacean vertebral column (backbone) extends into the center of the flukes, the flukes themselves are made of connective tissue like that in your outer ear and nose. This connective tissue makes the flukes both stiff and flexible.

Several species of whales are very large. The largest land animals ever to live were certain dinosaurs that were extinct long before whales came into existence. These dinosaurs may have reached over 100 feet (30 meters) in length and weighed up to 100 tons (91,000 kilo-

grams). They had massive, pillarlike bones that supported their weight and allowed them to move about on land.

Some species of cetaceans have evolved to weigh more than the largest dinosaur because their great weight is supported by water. How big are cetaceans? The smallest dolphins measure about 5 feet (1.5 meters) long and weigh 150 pounds (70 kilograms). They are dwarfed by the blue whale, which can be an astounding 100 feet (30 meters) long and can weigh up to 180 tons (160,000 kilograms). Just the tongue of a blue whale weighs as much as an entire African elephant, and a small child could crawl through the blue whale's largest blood vessel!

Moby Richard: What's in a Name?

Globicephala melas and *Globicephala macrorhynchus*—these are the scientific names for two closely related cetacean species commonly called ca'aing whale, pothead, blackfish, or pilot whale. The problem with common names is that, because they vary—like slang—from region to region and from language to language, one animal may have several different names. An extreme example of the confusion that can result is the name "dolphin," which refers to a fish, a restaurant delicacy, as well as to a cetacean. Because customers confused the fish with the cetacean and would not order "dolphin," most restaurants now list the fish by its Hawaiian name, *mahi mahi.*

Another problem with common names for cetaceans is that they come from whalers' terms and are based on size, not on how the animals are related. All cetaceans longer than 15 feet (5 meters) were called whales, and most smaller species were called dolphins or porpoises. For instance, the cetacean commonly called the killer "whale" is actually the largest member of the dolphin family, Delphinidae.

Given such confusion, it is easy to see why scientists use such long and hard-to-pronounce (but accurate) names. With scientific nomenclature, each species has its own unique name that is recognized in every language. Scientific names are always in Latin and often describe some attribute of the particular species. The white-beaked dolphin, for example, has a descriptive scientific name, *Langenorhynchus albirostris: albirostris* means white rostrum or beak. The animal commonly called either killer whale or orca is scientifically known only as *Orcinus orca;* the fear that humans used to have toward the killer whale is reflected in its scientific name, which roughly translates as "the whale from the realm of the dead."

The mahi mahi, which is sometimes called a dolphin, is a fish, not a cetacean. NATURAL HISTORY MUSEUM OF LOS ANGELES COUNTY MODEL; DAN WATSON.

II

EVOLUTION

RIGHT:

An early ancestor of cetaceans was a meat-eating animal called a mesonychid. Although it was a hoofed animal (the "claws" visible on this model are actually small hooves), the mesonychid probably looked more like a short-legged wolf than a horse or cow. NATURAL HISTORY MUSEUM OF LOS ANGELES COUNTY MODEL; DAN WATSON.

PAGES 22–23:

The fossilized 8-foot (2.5-meter) long skull of the extinct baleen whale Mixocetus elysius, which swam in the waters off southern California 10 to 11 million years ago.

LACM VP 882; DAN WATSON.

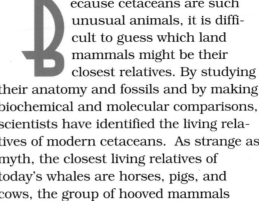

Because cetaceans are such unusual animals, it is difficult to guess which land mammals might be their closest relatives. By studying their anatomy and fossils and by making biochemical and molecular comparisons, scientists have identified the living relatives of modern cetaceans. As strange as myth, the closest living relatives of today's whales are horses, pigs, and cows, the group of hooved mammals called ungulates. We must look back about 50 million years to find the ancestor common to both whales and cows and to see how cetaceans have evolved.

Evolution is the process by which all living things change over time, usually in response to changes in the environment. Cetaceans evolved from an animal completely unlike the whales, dolphins, and porpoises of today. Their early ancestor was actually a land animal that walked on four legs, a meateater that resembled a short-legged wolf with hoof-like claws. This ancient animal is called a **mesonychid**.

Some mesonychids evolved into the most primitive group of whales, called the **archaeocetes**, meaning "ancient whales." Scientists believe that archaeocetes fed on fish. The smallest of the earliest whales were about 8 feet (2.5 meters) long; the largest were slender, eel-like animals measuring almost 60 feet (20 meters). Fossils of archaeocetes have been found around the world in such far apart locations as

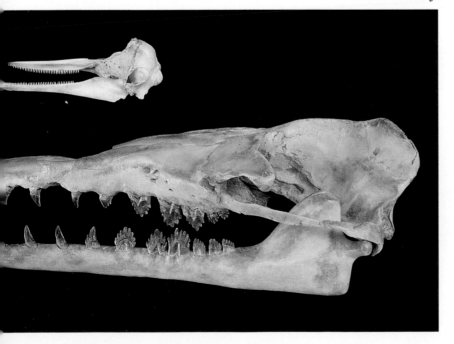

TOP:
An archaeocete, a descendant of the mesonychid and one of the first whales. Its feet are paddle-shaped, and its nose is not at the snout's tip but is closer to the top of the head. CYRENA NOUZILLE.

BOTTOM:
The relatively small skull of a modern dolphin compared with a cast of the skull of a 40-million-year-old archaeocete. The two are different in their teeth patterns and the positions of their noses. SKULL LACM 47143; DAN WATSON.

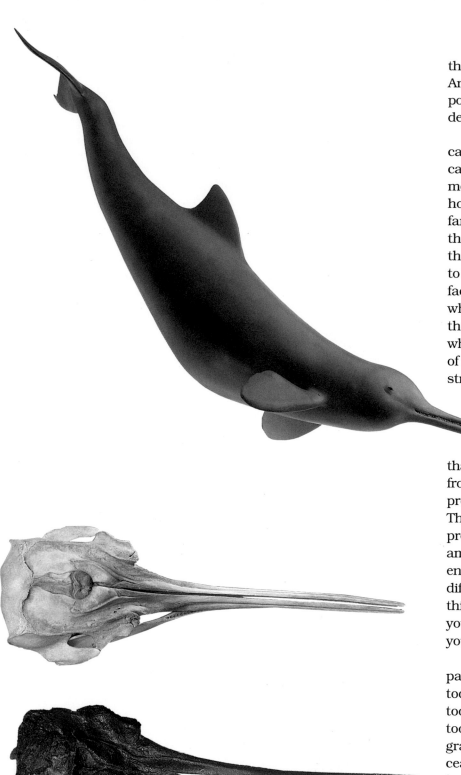

the southeastern United States, Egypt, Antarctica, and Pakistan, in sediments deposited when these land regions were under shallow seas.

The nose of mesonychids was located at the tip of the snout, in the typical position for a mammal. As some mesonychids evolved into archaeocetes, however, the position of the nose shifted farther and farther back, to the top of the head. With a nose closer to the top of the head, it was easier for early whales to breathe when they came to the surface. For millions of years, ancient whales had to stick their snouts out of the water to take a breath, but modern whales now have only to expose the top of their heads to breathe. We copy this strategy when we use a snorkel, a breathing tube that reaches from the top of our heads as we swim.

Archaeocetes had the same arrangement of teeth that exists in most mammals today. The front teeth were sharp and cone-shaped, probably for catching and holding fish. The back teeth were like blades to cut prey into bite-sized pieces. This is an example of a **heterodont** (meaning "different tooth") pattern, where an animal has different shaped teeth to do different things. People have a heterodont pattern: your front teeth are good for cutting, and your back teeth are good for grinding.

As archaeocetes evolved, their tooth patterns changed, and today most toothed whales have only one kind of tooth, a **homodont** (meaning "same tooth") pattern. They use their teeth for grabbing and piercing. Modern cetaceans don't chew their prey: they swallow it whole or tear it into pieces. Tooth size now varies among cetaceans depending on the particular prey that a species of whale or dolphin eats.

Ancient cetaceans may have spent some time on land, but by the late

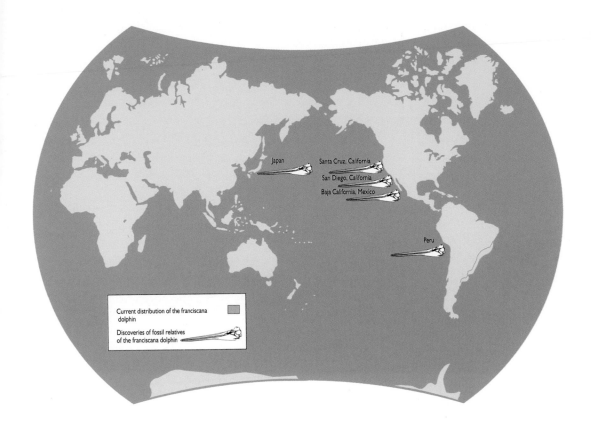

Current distribution of the franciscana dolphin

Discoveries of fossil relatives of the franciscana dolphin

Japan

Santa Cruz, California

San Diego, California

Baja California, Mexico

Peru

OPPOSITE, TOP:

The franciscana dolphin may have been given its name because of its color, which resembles that of the "gray friars" who were among the first European settlers of Uruguay.

NATURAL HISTORY MUSEUM OF LOS ANGELES COUNTY MODEL; DAN WATSON.

OPPOSITE, BOTTOM:

The skull of a modern franciscana dolphin (at top) and the cast of the very similar skull of an extinct relative found in California.

SKULL LACM 47143; DICK MEIER.

THIS PAGE:

Relatives of the franciscana were once widespread: 2 million years ago, they ranged along the Pacific coast from California to Peru and over to Japan. Today, the franciscana is found only along the Atlantic coast of South America, from Brazil to Argentina.

CYRENA NOUZILLE.

Eocene (about 40 million years ago), whales lacked hind limbs and had only paddlelike flippers for fore limbs—they could not have easily moved about on land. At some unknown point in their evolution, archaeocetes began to give birth in the water. This important milestone ended their ties to the land and freed them to live their entire lives in water.

The archaeocetes evolved into two groups, each with its own feeding method, and the two groups are still present today. The **baleen** whales, or **mysticetes**, filter tiny animals out of the water. Modern mysticetes include the blue, humpback, and gray whales. All mysticetes have two nostrils or blowholes. In contrast, the toothed whales, or **odontocetes**, have only one blowhole, eat larger prey, and have teeth—usually sharp and cone-shaped— to grab and hold their food. Killer whales, sperm whales, and all of the dolphins and porpoises are odontocetes.

Miocene Diversity

By the Miocene age (between 24 and 5 million years ago), there was a great abundance of cetaceans and many different species of both toothed whales and filter-feeding baleen whales. Early versions of all of the modern groups of cetaceans existed in the Miocene along with other types that are now extinct, such as the dolphin-sized squalodonts, predators with teeth like a shark's that disappeared about 6 million years ago.

Over time, evolution brings about changes in the shapes of animals and also in the number of species that exist and where each species lives. Habitats, the areas in which animals live, can change dramatically, in ways that may affect a particular species or all the

Natural Selection

The process by which organisms change over time, or **evolve,** is called natural selection. Charles Darwin first presented his theory of natural selection more than a hundred years ago, and all scientific evidence gathered since then has supported this theory.

The idea of natural selection is quite simple. Darwin first noticed that more young of a species are born than will survive into adulthood (before they can mature, some will be eaten, others will starve or die of disease). He also observed that individuals within the same species are a little different from each other (some are larger than others, some have sharper teeth than others, and so forth). Darwin speculated that most of these differences are inherited.

Darwin believed that these small differences give some individuals an advantage in the process of surviving to mature and have young (the expression "survival of the fittest" comes out of this idea), and that individuals with features best adapted to

the environment are more likely to be able to pass their successful traits on, through heredity, to the following generations. Darwin suggested that, over long periods of time, species themselves change as certain successful traits are "selected for" while other less successful features disappear.

The process of the selection of successful traits over time explains, for instance, how a land-dwelling mesonychid evolved into a cetacean. Scientists believe that some mesonychids began hunting along the shore, probably to catch fish. And that they may have begun to find more food in deeper waters or may have begun to escape from predators by swimming. Being able to swim better then meant being able to find more food and thus survive long enough to mate and reproduce. Poor swimmers may have found less food, and therefore have had fewer or no babies. So the genetic traits for living in the water were selected for, and some mesonychids evolved into fully aquatic primitive cetaceans.

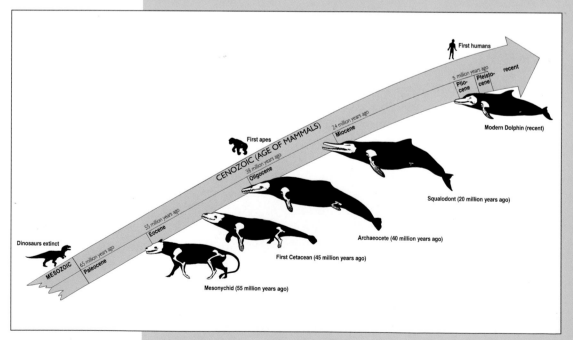

A geologic time line shows how the mesonychid's descendants may have made the transition from living on land to being fully aquatic. Through time,
• the nostrils moved to the top of the head and became blowholes, for quick breathing while swimming,
• the front legs became paddle-like flippers for steering, and the hind legs disappeared, • the tail widened into the horizontal flukes, for use in swimming, and • the body became sleek and streamlined for ease in moving through water. CYRENA NOUZILLE.

organisms living in an area. For example, the franciscana dolphin, which lives only in the nearshore waters along the east coast of South America from Brazil to Argentina, is the sole surviving member of a group of dolphin species that were common 7 to 2 million years ago. Fossils of this group have been found in what used to be coastal waters, from California south to Peru and across the Pacific to Japan, by paleontologists, the scientists who study fossils. As the habitat of this dolphin group changed, its members must have become extinct, one by one, until only the franciscana of the Atlantic Ocean remained.

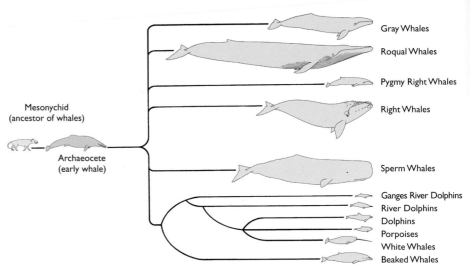

Modern Diversity

Of the 79 known species of cetaceans, 68 are odontocetes. These toothed whales range in size from the 60-foot (17-meter) sperm whale to the small franciscana dolphin and the finless porpoise, each less than 5 feet (1.5 meters) in length. Although there are only 11 species of baleen whales, they are quite diverse in size and shape. Mysticetes range in size from the 20-foot (6.1-meter) pygmy right whale to the 100-foot (30-meter) blue whale. The development of filter-feeding by the baleen whales put them on a completely different evolutionary path.

A feature that all toothed whales share is the ability to echolocate, to "see" their environment with sound. One common difference among them, however, is their color pattern. Many social species of dolphins that live in tropical waters, where water is clear, tend to have subtle color patterns. In such waters, it is probably easy to see other members of a pod at some distance, and subtle markings—such as the white tips on the snouts of adult male spotted dolphins—are easy to see from far away.

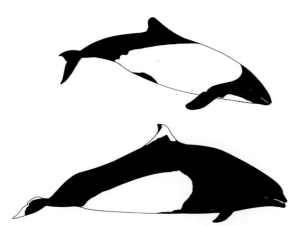

TOP:

The modern families of cetaceans and scientists' ideas about how they are related.
CYRENA NOUZILLE.

LEFT:

Commerson's dolphin (above) and Dall's porpoise.
CYRENA NOUZILLE.

Many social species that live in murky waters, where it's hard to see each other, have bold patterns of black and white. For example, the Dall's porpoise of the North Pacific, the Commerson's dolphin from the southern waters of South America, and the killer whale are all black and white. This striking color contrast may help members of each species see others of their kind in murky waters. These three species are not closely related, so the bold color pattern they share is a good example of convergent evolution.

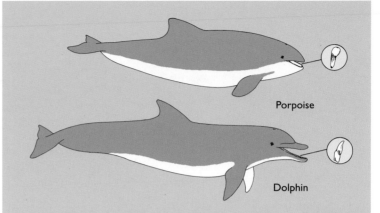

Porpoise

Dolphin

CYRENA NOUZILLE

IDENTITY CRISIS: DOLPHIN OR PORPOISE?

What is the difference between a dolphin and a porpoise? "Dolphin" usually refers to the specific group of small, toothed cetaceans in the family Delphinidae. There are over 30 species of true dolphins, including familiar species like the bottlenose, spinner, and spotted dolphins. Although the largest members of this group are commonly called whales because of their size, they are actually most closely related to other dolphins. The large dolphins include killer whales and pilot whales.

"Porpoise" refers to six species in the family Phocoenidae. All porpoises are relatively small by cetacean standards, measuring 7 feet (2 meters) or less as adults.

The notable differences between dolphins and porpoises are these:

Dolphins	*Porpoises*
● Always have cone-shaped teeth	● Always have spade-shaped teeth
● Usually have a beak	● Never have a beak
● Usually have a hooked or curved dorsal fin (some have no dorsal fin)	● Usually have a dorsal fin shaped like a triangle (some have no dorsal fin)

TOP:

This blue whale has the two blowholes typical of all baleen whales. JOHN E. HEYNING.

LEFT:

The bottlenose dolphin, like all other toothed whales, has a single blowhole. JOHN E. HEYNING.

III

LIFE BELOW THE SURFACE

All animals share the need to behave in ways that will keep them alive. One characteristic of all living beings, including cetaceans, is that they must eat! Many features of an animal's body and patterns of behavior are related to what it eats and how it goes about finding a meal. After years of scientific research, people are now beginning to understand how the adaptations of a dolphin or a whale help it to prosper in its aquatic environment.

Feeding

Cetaceans are carnivorous, or meat-eating, but the size of their prey varies tremendously. Killer whales may eat prey as large as a blue whale, while some baleen whales feed on animals that are almost microscopic. Baleen and toothed whales are mostly different in what they eat and how they locate and capture their food.

The mysticetes' baleen consists of long, narrow plates, each with a fringe-like inner surface; the plates hang down from their upper jaws like vertical window blinds. Baleen is made of **keratin,** like human hair and fingernails. Mysticetes use their baleen to filter tiny animals from the water. Surprisingly, these enormous whales have a menu that consists entirely of small fish and the animals in the **plankton**, the small organisms that drift in the ocean's currents.

Instead of hunting a few large animals, mysticetes filter out thousands of small prey all at once, using their baleen. A baleen whale first opens its mouth and takes in a huge mouthful of water. It then partially closes its mouth and forces the water out between its baleen plates. The prey is caught against the fringed surface of the baleen. Filtered this way from the water, hundreds of small animals are captured in the ba-

leen and then swallowed. A single meal for a blue whale may weigh up to 2 tons (2,000 kilograms)!

Baleen whales won't eat just anything. They often seek out a particular prey and ignore other types of food. As a group, they have several methods of "shopping" for a meal: skimming, gulping, or sucking. Each method is best to capture a particular prey.

Right whales and bowhead whales are famous for their skimming technique. With mouths wide open, they swim along the surface with their long baleen plates exposed. This feeding technique is excellent for capturing small, surface-dwelling plankton, which typically cannot move fast enough to avoid the slowly swimming whale.

The gulpers—the humpback, blue whale, and their relatives, the **rorquals**—are the whales that have many grooves extending from their chins back beyond their throats. These throat grooves expand like the pleats of a skirt, turning the whale's mouth into a huge sack. The whale gulps a large volume of water into this giant sack, then forces the water out, trapping the prey inside. Gulping is an effective way to catch prey that swim fast, such as small schooling fish or **krill**, the shrimp-like plankton abundant in Antarctic waters.

For sucking mud, the gray whale is the only champion. It swims on its side along the ocean bottom, vacuuming up mud and water. It then filters the sediment through its baleen, which have short, stiff fringes, good at straining out $1/2$- to 2-inch (2- to 5-centimeter) crustaceans from the mud. Gray whales leave a trail on the ocean bottom—great craters where they have sucked and slurped their meals.

To find enough food, most mysticetes must follow their prey and

LEFT:
A killer whale eats a salmon. Some populations of killer whales feed on fish; others specialize in marine mammal prey.
KELLEY BALCOMB-BARTOK/
MARINE MAMMAL IMAGES.

PAGES 32–33:
The eye of a gray whale. Most whales have good eyesight; but because visibility in the ocean is so poor, a large whale may not be able to see its tail.
HOWARD HALL/HOWARD HALL
PRODUCTIONS.

TOP:

Cast of the head of a minke whale, showing baleen hanging from its upper jaw. The minke and other baleen whales use the baleen to filter small fish and plankton from the water. CAST OF LACM 88944; DAN WATSON.

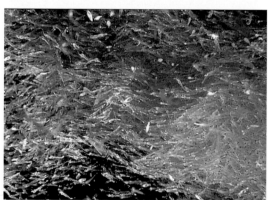

RIGHT:

One of the most abundant forms of plankton is krill, a group of shrimp-like crustaceans. A single species of krill provides much of the food for all of the marine mammals and penguins in the Antarctic. MARK CONLIN/HOWARD HALL PRODUCTIONS.

OPPOSITE:

Right whales feed by skimming the water's surface. Their baleen is finely fringed to filter tiny prey out of the water. FLIP NICKLIN, MINDEN PICTURES.

BLOWING BUBBLES AT DINNER

Some humpback whales have developed a variation on the gulping style of feeding. They swim in circles far below the surface and release air from their blowholes to create a curtain of bubbles called a bubble-net. The prey are frightened by the bubbles and gather close together in the center of the bubble-net. The whales then swim up through the center of the net, mouths open, and capture the neatly collected prey.

In some regions, instead of a circle of bubbles, the humpbacks produce a single blast of bubbles, which also confuses and frightens the prey.

TOP:

The throat of a blue whale with its mouth full of water. Blue whales and their rorqual relatives can consume entire schools of small fish or swarms of plankton by taking in a single huge gulp of water. When these whales gulp in, their pleated throats expand. MARK CONLIN/HOWARD HALL PRODUCTIONS.

BOTTOM:

Like giant vacuum cleaners, gray whales suck mud up from the sea floor and then filter the bottom-dwelling amphipods out of it. FLIP NICKLIN, MINDEN PICTURES.

MITUAKI IWAGO

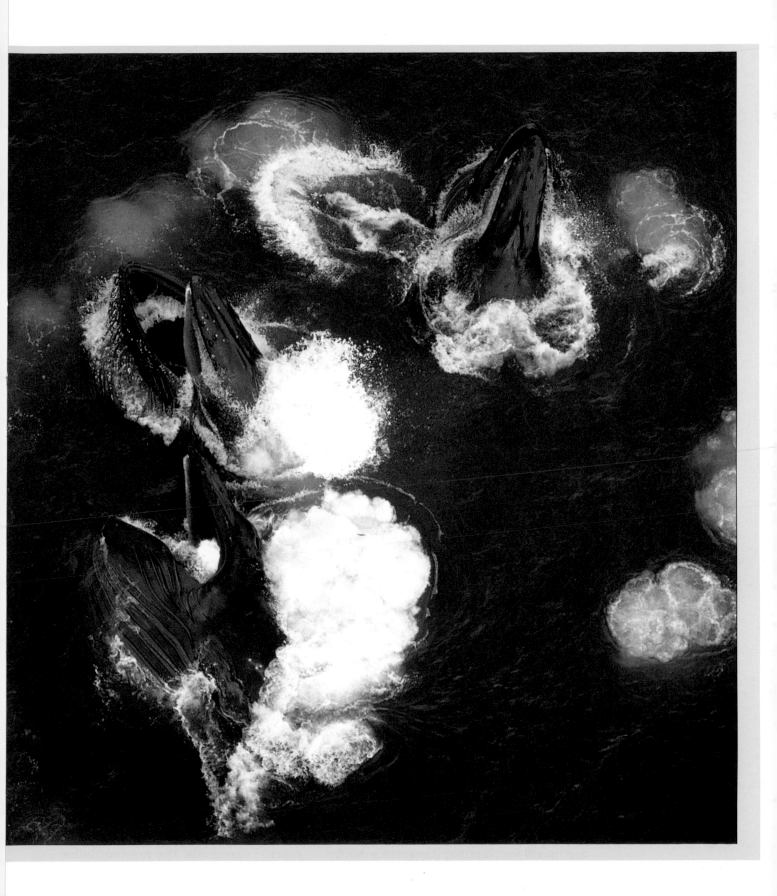

chase their prey because the fish they hunt can't hear the high-frequency sounds of their pursuers.

To see how cetaceans interact with other species of animals and plants in their habitats, it is useful to look at the larger picture of who eats what. Every animal eats something and is later eaten by something else. Plants form the basis of food on this planet by obtaining the energy they need from the sun. **Herbivores** are animals that feed on plants to get the energy they need to live, grow, and reproduce. On land, there are both small herbivores, such as snails and mice, and large herbivores, such as deer and cows. **Carnivores,** the meat-eaters, are animals that eat other animals; they include whales, lions, hawks, and spiders, both large and small animals. People and other animals that eat both plants and animals are called **omnivores**.

Imagine a **food pyramid** formed by plants and animals. Plants form the base and are eaten by herbivores, which are eaten by carnivores. This food pyramid is also a pyramid of energy. Energy from the sun is converted into plants. The energy from plants is used by herbivores and then by carnivores. In this food or energy pyramid, there are many plants, fewer herbivores, and even fewer carnivores. This is because higher on the pyramid, energy is more and more concentrated into fewer and fewer individuals. For example, in the food (or energy) pyramid, it takes 1,000 pounds (450 kilograms) of plants to make 100 pounds (45 kilograms) of herbivore; it takes 100 pounds of herbivore to make 10 pounds (4.5 kilograms) of small carnivore; and 10 pounds of small carnivore are needed to produce 1 pound of large carnivore. The higher up on the

pyramid, the less food is available. This is why large carnivores are rare.

A similar food pyramid is found in the marine environment, but one difference is the size of the plants. Most plants in the ocean are microscopic plant plankton, which are eaten by small animal plankton. Many of the animal plankton are **crustaceans**, the group that includes crabs and shrimp. Many ocean carnivores, including small fish and squid, feed on animal plankton. Small fish and squid are eaten by larger fish and larger squid, which are then eaten by even larger fish and marine mammals. Killer whales are at the top of this pyramid, feeding on large fish or other marine mammals. Because they are "top carnivores," there are relatively few killer whales in the world's oceans; the same is true for other large ocean carnivores, like many species of sharks.

Where do baleen whales belong in

OPPOSITE:
Squid do not stand a chance against the pilot whale's short, blunt jaws and widely spaced teeth.
JOHN E. HEYNING.

ABOVE:
Most small dolphins, like this short-beaked common dolphin, have long, slender jaws with many sharp teeth, which they use to capture fish and squid.
LACM 84134; JOHN E. HEYNING.

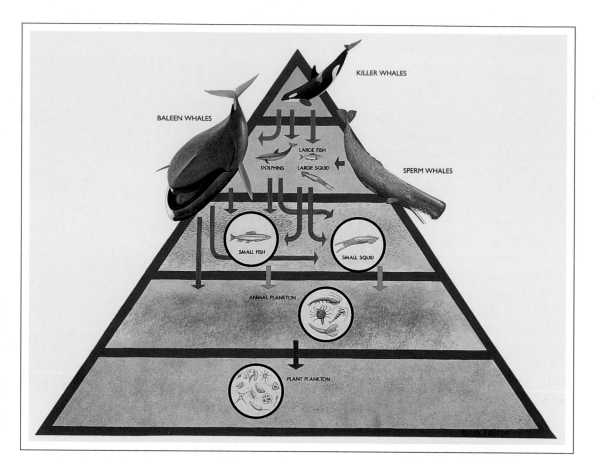

A marine food pyramid. It seems amazing that the largest whales, the baleen whales, feed on tiny animal plankton or small fish. But these whales are "feeding low on the food pyramid" because the prey are much more plentiful there. LARRY FOSTER.

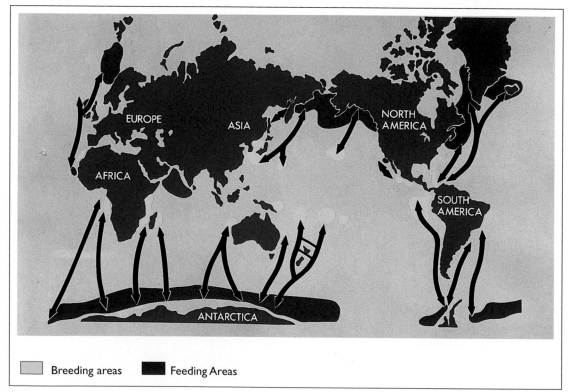

Migration routes of humpback whales. Most baleen whales migrate to cold waters for the summer, to take advantage of the plankton blooms there, and then migrate to the tropics in the winter to breed and calve.
CYRENA NOUZILLE.

Breeding areas Feeding Areas

the food pyramid? Baleen whales are unique in that, unlike other large carnivores, they feed on small planktonic animals and fish low on the food pyramid. Baleen whales can grow to enormous size and large numbers because of their abundant food source. Interestingly, the largest sharks—the basking and whale sharks—feed in the same low position in the food pyramid as do the great whales.

Senses

Whales and dolphins have evolved senses that serve them well in the ocean's changing conditions of clear to cloudy water, warm to cold temperatures, and surface to deep waters. They see, touch, hear, and taste so that they can navigate, find food, avoid predators, and find mates in their fluid world.

Anyone who has gone swimming or diving in the ocean notices that it is difficult to see beyond several feet. At best, in clear tropical water, visibility may be only a few hundred feet (around 50 meters). Although most cetaceans have good vision, many of the larger whales often cannot even see the distance of their own body length because of murky water.

In the ocean, light penetrates only to about 600 feet (200 meters), yet many odontocetes dive far deeper into dark waters and are still able to find prey. Some deep-diving whales and dolphins are perhaps aided in their search for food by **bioluminescence**—the light that some organisms generate using specialized organs. Many deepwater species of fish and squid have bioluminescent organs to attract mates or lure prey. Whales might see and use this light to locate dinner. Even stranger, some fish and squid may be attracted to bioluminiscent light reflected off the white teeth and mouths of many deep-diving cetaceans.

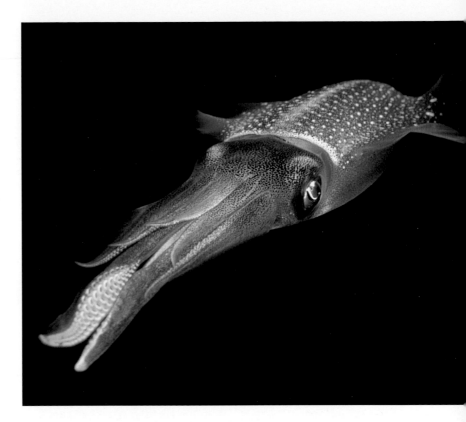

Many species of fish and squid produce their own light, called bioluminescence, to attract mates or prey.
HOWARD HALL/HOWARD HALL PRODUCTIONS.

Ganges river dolphins of India cannot see well at all. Because their eyes do not have functional lenses, they cannot see images but probably can detect changes in light and dark. The waters in which they live are so murky that good eyesight would be useless. But many dolphins that live in clear water, like the spinner, spotted and bottlenose dolphins, have excellent eyesight and probably use it mostly to keep track of each other.

Fish rely heavily on smell, yet cetaceans—unlike other mammals—have little if any sense of smell. Why do whales, dolphins, and porpoises lack this important sense? Mammals smell by bringing air—with all its interesting odors—in through their noses while they breathe. But breathing occurs infrequently for whales and dolphins and only above water. Because cetaceans do not have an opportunity to detect odors under water, they have apparently, over time, lost the sense of smell.

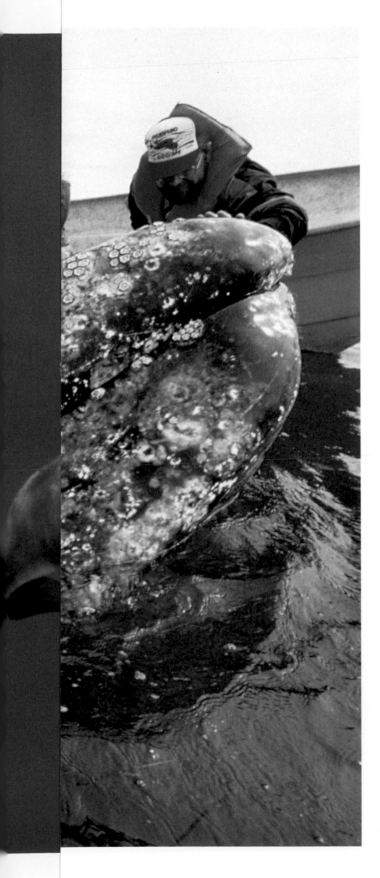

WHAT'S YOUR NAME?

Among the many sounds it makes, each bottlenose dolphin also produces its own whistle! Scientists believe that **signature whistles,** unique to each individual, may be like names, allowing dolphins to identify each other by sound. When one bottlenose dolphin whistles its own signature, another dolphin often mimics or repeats it, perhaps as a way of acknowledging the other's presence. A newborn bottlenose quickly develops its own whistle, which is necessary to its becoming a member of dolphin society.

Sperm whales produce individual patterns of echolocation clicks called **codas.** We know very little about how sperm whales use these codas or if they are like signature whistles. Perhaps other toothed whales also produce sounds that function as names.

Scientists use a recorder with a suction cup to listen to the sounds that dolphins make underwater. PETER TYACK, WOODS HOLE OCEANOGRAPHIC INSTITUTION.

LEFT:
The sense of touch is well developed among whales, dolphins, and porpoises. This gray whale may be "friendly" because it enjoys having people touch its skin. FLIP NICKLIN, MINDEN PICTURES.

A pil
Who
their
food,
locat
wate.

WHY DON'T CETACEANS GET THE BENDS?

When scuba diving, we cannot dive too deeply or too long or we will get the "bends," a condition that causes people to bend over in pain. In a dive, pressure on the body increases, and nitrogen in the pressurized air we breathe while scuba diving dissolves into our blood stream and tissues. If we dive too far down or stay under for too long, too much nitrogen will be dissolved into our bodies. If we surface too quickly, the nitrogen forms bubbles in our blood, like the bubbles formed when we open a bottle of soda pop. Symptoms of the bends range from pain in the joints to death.

Cetaceans dive so much deeper and longer than humans—how do they avoid this misery? First of all, when under water, cetaceans are not breathing pressurized air as is the scuba diver. The cetacean holds its breath under water, breathing only at the surface, so there is not a constant supply of new pressurized air to be dissolved into its body. Scientists think that the deepest diving cetaceans may actually exhale before diving so that they have less air in their lungs to be dissolved under pressure.

Amazingly, when a cetacean dives deep, under tons of pressure, its lungs actually collapse because there is no new supply of air to pump them up.

FLIP NICKLIN, MINDEN PICTURES

---

in an environment where sight is limited and where most prey can't hear high-frequency sounds. In experiments, dolphins have been able to detect a 3-inch (10-centimeter) ball at a distance of almost 300 feet (100 meters.) That is like a person being able to see a tennis ball at the far end of a football field!

Within its head, off the nasal passages under the blowhole, a toothed whale has a series of elaborate sacs. By moving air back and forth between the sacs, it produces the sounds needed for echolocation. In its forehead is a fatty organ called the **melon**, where scientists believe the echolocation sounds are focused. The echo reflects back to the its ear via the lower jaw. Some researchers believe that toothed whales can focus and produce echolocation sounds loud enough to actually stun their prey! Even though toothed whales can echolocate whenever they want to, they will often hunt silently, using only their very good hearing to detect their noisy prey.

Cetaceans produce some sounds that are either too low or too high for us to hear. The toothed whales' higher frequency sounds provide the most detailed information. Most large baleen whales produce very low-frequency sounds, which are able to travel long distances. With these low-frequency sounds, it is possible that baleen whales can communicate across hundreds of miles.

OPPOSITE:
A gray whale spyhops in a Baja California lagoon.
HOWARD HALL/HOWARD HALL PRODUCTIONS.

supply oxygen to their vital organs by shutting down the blood flow to parts of the body that do not need a constant supply of oxygen, such as the muscles and other organs. This ability to **shunt** blood is critical to a cetacean's diving feats.

Behavior and Social Systems

We know very little about the behavior and social systems of most cetaceans. Most of their activities occur beneath the ocean's surface, far from the watchful eyes of people. But scientists have now compiled long-term observations on certain species, including humpback, killer, sperm, and right whales and bottlenose and spinner dolphins. With the use of advanced technology, biologists have begun to understand certain kinds of whale and dolphin behavior and to unravel some secrets of cetacean society.

A group of whales is called a **pod**, an old whalers' term, and a group of dolphins or porpoises is called either a **school** or a pod. Some cetaceans are highly social, living in large and complex pods. Others are solitary or form groups only for short periods of time.

Whether social or solitary, some whales and dolphins share certain kinds of behavior. When a whale leaps from the water and falls back in with a resounding splash, we say it is **breaching**. The humpback whale is well known for such acrobatic displays. Scientists are not sure whether breaching is a social behavior. Theories about breaching include the idea that the whale is trying to rid itself of parasites by slapping its body against the water's surface, or that breaching is a form of communication intended for nearby whales.

When a whale or dolphin raises its head almost vertically out of the water

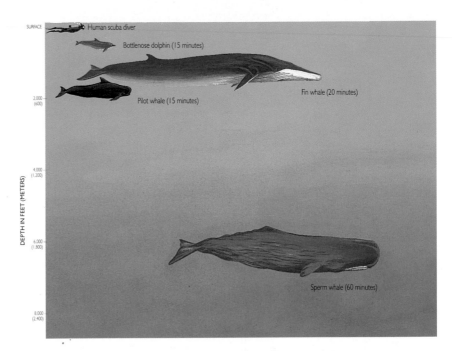

for a short period of time, we call the behavior **spyhopping**. The term originated with whalers, who believed that the whales are spying when they peer above the water. Perhaps they are!

When a cetacean raises its flukes and slaps the water's surface, it is **lobtailing**. This is thought to show irritation, or to be an aggressive display, at least in humpback whales, bottlenose dolphins, and killer whales.

Anyone who has seen a group of dolphins speed along in front of a ship has been awed by their grace and speed. As a boat moves through the water, it pushes ahead of it a pressure wave of water called a bow wave. Dolphins can place themselves in this wave and **bowride**. In the right position, a dolphin can even stop swimming and merely be pushed along. Biologists believe that boat bowriding is an extension of the dolphins' "bowriding" of large whales! This behavior may be learned by young dolphins as they are pulled along in the current created by their swimming mothers. The reason for bowriding is not clear, but it may represent a behavior many mammals enjoy—play!

Depths and durations of cetacean dives are given here (the number in parentheses is the maximum length of time that the animal can spend under water). CYRENA NOUZILLE.

OPPOSITE:
Dolphins swim into the bow wave of a boat to bowride.
BOB TALBOT.

55

The organization of toothed whale societies depends in part on where they live. For example, river dolphins usually live alone or in very small groups. Nearshore or shallow-water species live in pods of only a few individuals. In contrast, the ocean-going dolphins such as the spotted and spinner dolphins form immense schools of hundreds or even thousands of members.

The pods of bottlenose dolphins off Florida are usually made up of females and their offspring. Both male and female **subadults** ("teenagers") leave their groups, but females usually return to their mother's group when they bear their first calf. A male finds another male about his age and the two stay together as buddies, sometimes for life. Males travel outside the limited **home range** of the female groups, but they do join with the female groups for short periods of time, probably to mate. Like human societies, dolphin societies may vary; what occurs with dolphins along the coast of Florida may not occur in groups of dolphins living somewhere else.

Recent research on pilot whales around the Faroe Islands north of Great Britain and off the Canary Islands in the Northeast Atlantic reveals a different type of cetacean society. Scientists analyzed DNA from the Faroe Island pilot whales and found that the males within a pod are usually not the fathers of the pod's calves. Biologists believe that two or more pods come together for brief periods of time so that males of one group can mate with females of another group. In pilot whale societies, the males and females may never leave their mother's pod, but by breeding with members of other pods, they avoid mating with a close relative. Pilot whales, like many mammals (including humans), are **sexually dimorphic**—the sexes look different. Male pilot whales

PAGES 56–57:
Humpback whales make spectacular breaches.
FLIP NICKLIN, MINDEN PICTURES.

OPPOSITE:
A pod of pilot whales. A male stays in its mother's pod all its life, leaving only to mate with females in other pods. The older females in a pod no longer reproduce but may help to raise the calves of their relatives. BOB TALBOT.

Some cetaceans, such as these long-beaked common dolphins, are highly social and live in large groups. Pods of common dolpins can number over a thousand individuals. JOHN E. HEYNING.

PAGES 62–63:

Bottlenose dolphins live in very complex social groups. FLIP NICKLIN, MINDEN PICTURES.

What a Difference! Sexual Dimorphism

In many animals, there are great physical differences between males and females; **sexual dimorphism** is the term given to such differences. Examples include the antlers on male deer or the larger size and hairy mane of the male lion.

Some cetaceans, especially the toothed whales, exhibit unusual extremes of sexual dimorphism. Only the male narwhal grows the 9-foot (2.7-meter) twisting tusk. Only male beaked whales have one or two pairs of lower-jaw teeth that grow to large size. In one species, the strap-toothed whale, the male's teeth actually grow over the upper jaw like two straps! In sperm whales, adults males may weigh up to three times more than females. The opposite is true for the baleen whales, where the females are slightly larger than the males.

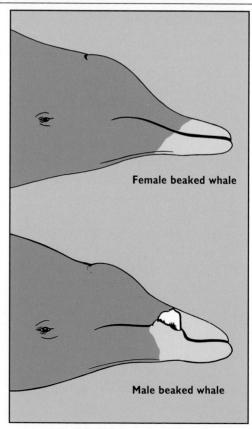

Female beaked whale

Male beaked whale

ing as those of some toothed whales. Certain rorqual whales, especially humpback, do come together in groups to work cooperatively to get food.

In their tropical grounds, male humpbacks sing long and loud. Their songs are repeated units of sound that may last from 2 to 20 minutes. The songs may be used to declare territories to other males, or to lure females, or for both purposes. One theory is that the length of a male's song shows how long he can go without taking a breath of air and is proof of how strong and healthy he is. A male humpback's song may be his advertisement that he would make a good mate!

The song of the humpback whale is different from most bird song. Instead of singing the same song year after year as birds do, humpbacks change their songs every season, adding and deleting portions of the songs, perhaps as part of the competition for females. When they leave the breeding grounds to migrate to feeding areas, the males usually stop singing. The next winter, when the humpbacks return to the breeding region, they begin singing again, at first using the version of the song that they were singing at the end of the last breeding season. It is as though they pick up again from where they left off last year!

The calves of baleen whales are weaned when they are 7 months to 1 year old, much sooner than the calves of toothed whales. Some scientists think that the reason a toothed whale spends more time with its mother is that it takes longer for a calf to learn the social skills of its more complex society.

Many people believe that whales and dolphins live in constant social harmony: perhaps the perpetual smile of the dolphin gives us this impression. While some members of a dolphin species may take care of a sick or injured member of the pod, most dolphins and whales are also sometimes aggressive. Aggression establishes the pecking order within the pod and decides who mates with whom in the breeding season. Scars on the bodies of cetaceans of all ages and species show that whales and dolphins can and do fight with each other.

Humpback whales are among the most aggressive of the baleen whales, especially during their mating seasons. A male humpback, called an "escort," will often accompany a female that has recently given birth and is probably ready to mate again. The escort fights vigorously with other males that attempt to get close to the female by thrashing his tail side to side or lobtailing. Male humpbacks sometimes ram other males with their heads, which are covered with sharp barnacles that can cut the skin of their rivals.

Beaked whales are a little known group of toothed whales with 19 species ranging from 14 to 40 feet (3.5 to 12 meters) in length. Most species are quite sexually dimorphic. The teeth of females in most species of beaked whales never erupt from the gums, and their bodies are relatively free of scars. But the males of these species have at least one pair of large teeth in the lower jaw that erupt

PAGE 66-67:
A male humpback whale (lower left), called an escort, will often accompany a female that has recently given birth and is ready to mate again. FLIP NICKLIN, MINDEN PICTURES.

The bloody fin on this male humpback resulted when it was rammed by a rival male, which used the sharp barnacle growths on its head as a weapon, to break skin. FLIP NICKLIN, MINDEN PICTURES.

65

IV

THE CHALLENGES OF RESEARCH

PAGES 70–71:

Scientists from the Natural History Museum of Los Angeles County prepare to take tissue samples and collect the skull of a dead humpback whale that has washed ashore in southern California.

LACM 91353; RICHARD ROSS.

It is rare to see narwhals fencing or humpbacks mating. Conducting scientific research on animals that swim fast, spend their lives below the surface, and dive deep is very difficult. But scientists are beginning to piece together a picture of the lives of cetaceans like a giant jigsaw puzzle—an observation here, an experiment or theory there. The methods used to unlock these mysteries are as fascinating as the questions asked. How do researchers study cetaceans?

Tagging/Photo-identification

Scientists have for a long time found it useful not just to observe groups of animals but to try to follow the actions of specific individuals over a period of time. But with cetaceans, this can be like watching a soccer game where all the players are wearing exactly the same uniform. Biologists who want to study individual whales and dolphins need a way to tell the animals apart— they need something like the numbers on soccer players' shirts.

Years ago, when researchers first began to study individual cetaceans, they placed a tag on each animal so it could easily be identified. This required capturing each whale or dolphin and putting on a tag while avoiding any harm to the animal. Attaching tags was difficult and limited the number of animals that could be studied. Imagine trying to hold and tag a 100-foot (30-meter) long blue whale!

Now most scientists use "natural tags"—marks such as the color patterns on a whale's body or the unique profiles of the flukes or dorsal fin. Researchers take a series of pictures of wild cetaceans and compare the photographs to those taken previously, using natural

Scientists can recognize individual whales by natural markings, such as the color patterns and shapes of the flukes of these humpback whales. By comparing photographs of the natural "tags" taken at different places and times, they can sometimes trace the movements of an individual. FLIP NICKLIN, MINDEN PICTURES *(TOP)* AND NATIONAL MARINE MAMMAL LABORATORY.

The Mystery of Mass Strandings

Why would a group of dolphins or whales strand themselves on the beach and die? Such mass strandings have perplexed humans for ages. Many explanations have been proposed: perhaps the leader of a pod is sick and the others follow it to their deaths. Perhaps parasites in the brain cause the whales to lose their ability to navigate. Maybe polluted water is poisoning the animals.

Although pollution may be a problem in many areas, it alone does not explain mass strandings, which are known to have occurred even prior to the industrial revolution, when pollution became a problem. There also do not seem to be more mass strandings in polluted areas than in clean areas. Although some parasites do get into cetaceans' brains and cause a lot of damage, parasites alone do not explain mass strandings. Individual dolphins or whales may die from parasites, but it is unlikely that an entire pod would become infected all at the same time.

One recent idea on strandings is that cetaceans, like many other animals, may be able to detect and use the earth's magnetic field to navigate. Near some shores, the rocks below the ocean floor cause the magnetic field to be distorted. In such regions, whales or dolphins could make navigational errors, get confused, and strand themselves. This might explain why there are many mass strandings in some areas and none in others.

Another theory has to do with cetacean society, especially in toothed whales. When a mass stranding occurs, the close social ties of the pod may actually be dangerous. At sea, these animals stay together to protect themselves. In a stranding, animals still capable of swimming away may not be able to abandon their tightly linked pod. The unfortunate result would be stranding of all the group members, including perfectly healthy animals, which would then quickly die from stress or overheating on the beach.

In June 1979 a pod of sperm whales stranded and died on Florence Beach in Oregon. JIM LARISON/OREGON SEA GRANT.

tags to identify individuals. Photo-identification has been particularly useful in studying bottlenose dolphins, humpback whales, right whales, and killer whales.

Information from photo-identification studies can tell us the migration routes of individuals and whether the same individuals return to a certain spot each year. Long-term studies can reveal if individual females have a new calf every year or every few years and whether or not the calves survive. Feeding style, aggressive behavior, and long-term associations among individuals can also be determined by photo-identification.

Two bottlenose dolphins bear several kinds of tags.
FLIP NICKLIN, MINDEN PICTURES.

The development of miniature electronic devices has given rise to computer tags. These new instruments collect specific information about the tagged whale and store it on tiny computers; it can then be transmitted to a nearby ship or a passing satellite. The tags can tell how deep and how long a whale dives as well as the animal's position at a given time. This new space-age technology allows scientists a glimpse into the secret lives of cetaceans far beneath the waves.

Strandings

When most people see a stranded whale or dolphin on the beach, they are saddened by the death of such a large and graceful creature. But the lifeless carcass can provide a wealth of information about how that animal lived. By studying many stranded animals, biologists can piece together basic information about the size, shape, color, sex, prey, and geographical range of a mysterious species.

Scientists classify strandings as single strandings, mass strandings, and mass mortalities. Single strandings— one animal beaching itself—are the

SCIENCE SLEUTHS

Like modern-day detectives, scientists are always looking for the answers to questions. The first step in this process is usually to observe something that provokes a question that can be answered by research.

For example, scientists noticed that some members of the common dolphin species (*Delphinus delphis*) had very long beaks and some had shorter beaks. Because members of a certain species are never identical to each other, the scientists asked a question: "Are the differences in beak length a sign that there are two species here, or does this difference just represent normal variation within one species?"

Having asked the question, scientists then carefully collect and analyze information, or data, to answer it. Differences between individuals of the same species can be because of age, sex, and geographic region, so scientists studying a species need to examine many animals. This is why natural history museums, where questions about species are investigated, collect large numbers of specimens.

Scientists also need to look at many features. To answer the dolphin beak question, scientists measured entire bodies, skulls, and color patterns of many dolphins to get the most information possible. Other researchers looked at DNA for an answer as to whether there are one or two species of common dolphin.

Once the information has been collected and analyzed, the scientist has results which can be used to come to a conclusion. In the dolphin example, some results did not help answer the question. For example, the number of teeth in longer- and shorter-nosed common dolphins varied widely. Other results, however, like the snout measurements, color pattern comparisons, and DNA analyses, provided evidence that there are definitely two species of common dolphins. The researchers named them *Delphinus delphis* and *Delphinus capensis*—short-beaked and long-beaked common dolphins.

Scientists publish the results of their research in technical articles so that other scientists can read the details and evaluate the research. This information may then be published in newspapers, magazines, and popular books, where any interested reader can learn the results of valuable research.

At the end of most studies, scientists find even more questions to be asked, and the process of research continues.

most common event. Mass strandings, where many animals of the same species strand together, are rather rare and tend to occur in certain areas. In a mass mortality, many animals (sometimes of more than one species) die and strand over a short period of time, usually weeks or months.

Whatever the cause of the stranding, many things—like an animal's age—can be discovered from examining the carcass. The age of a toothed whale can be determined by cutting a tooth lengthwise and counting the layers inside, like counting the growth rings of a tree. To learn the age of a baleen whale (which, of course, lacks teeth), biologists remove the wax plug from the ear canal and count the layers in the wax. By combining age information with other data, it is possible to determine the age at which males and females become mature as well as the average life expectancy for the species.

The reproductive organs of a stranded animal can tell us about a species' breeding behavior. The testes of males or the ovaries of females show if the animal was mature or immature. With information from a series of strandings, the breeding and calving season of a species can be determined.

How Many Species?

Even after centuries of studying and observing whales, we are still not sure exactly how many species of cetaceans exist today. A new species of beaked whale from the eastern Pacific was recently discovered when several animals from the species were caught in fishing nets. Sometimes a certain species, such as the spinner dolphin, is found to actually be two or more closely related species.

Each species of animal is recognized by its ability to reproduce only with others of its kind. The work of identifying species of plants and animals and the

THE MARINE MAMMAL RESEARCH LABORATORY

In southern California, when a whale dies after stranding on the beach or when a cetacean's body washes ashore, authorities know to call the curators at the Natural History Museum of Los Angeles County. Dead animals are a valuable source of knowledge for scientists, and the Natural History Museum's marine mammal biologists actively investigate all reports of cetacean strandings. The information collected is used to understand the natural history and evolution of whales and dolphins, to promote their conservation, and to educate the public about these amazing marine mammals.

The museum's Marine Mammal Laboratory houses the world's second largest research collection of marine mammals. This collection is used by biologists from the museum and all over the world. Because the collection contains many specimens of some species, scientists are able to piece together the natural history of these species, including their distribution, reproductive biology, and feeding ecology. The detailed dissections of cetaceans that are performed in the lab provide insights into how whales' and dolphins' bodies work (for example, how dolphins produce sounds); these examinations also help to determine how cetaceans evolved and how the different species are related to each other. Over the years, hundreds of research projects have been based on specimens housed in the museum's collections.

Understanding the biology of animals and the ecosystems in which they live is a crucial step in ensuring their future survival. The Natural His-

tory Museum's Marine Mammal Laboratory keeps records on the impact that the fishing industry has on whales and dolphins. The tissues that we collect are used to determine

the levels of pollutants— such as DDT— in marine animals. And DNA samples taken from specimens in our collection have aided in the identification of meat from endangered species of whales that are being hunted illegally in remote parts of the world.

OPPOSITE:
Baleen whale skulls in storage in the Marine Mammal Research Laboratory. RICHARD ROSS.

ABOVE:
Tissue samples as well as skeletons are kept in the laboratory for analyses for trace contaminants and DNA patterns. RICHARD ROSS.

LEFT:
The larvae of dermestid beetles help museum curators prepare marine mammal skeletons for storage: the larvae eat the last bits of meat off the bones and, because of their size, are able to clean areas that would be hard to reach with tools or fingers. RICHARD ROSS.

relationships between species is the science of **systematics**. Biologists who study systematics try to determine which differences between organisms are due to age, sex, or geographical location, and which differences separate one species from another.

For several hundred years, information for systematics studies of cetaceans has come from measuring and comparing whole animals, parts of skeletons, and color patterns. Stranded animals provide most of the specimens for this type of research.

New genetic techniques now help biologists to identify species, and groups within species, by analyzing genetic material. DNA can be collected from wild whales by using a retrievable dart that removes a small sample of skin and blubber without harming the animal. Samples of blood collected during brief capture-and-release operations can also provide DNA, as can tissues taken

ABOVE:
The beached carcass of a newborn gray whale is loaded on the Natural History Museum's whale retrieval truck for transport to the museum. LACM 88980; JOHN E. HEYNING.

LEFT:
Museum paleontologists work to uncover the skeleton of a 100,000-year-old fossil gray whale. LACM VP 122322; LARRY REYNOLDS.

from dead stranded animals.

It is important to be able to identify all cetacean species so that we can protect and conserve them. But to protect any species, we must protect its **populations**. A population (or **stock** or **subspecies**) is a group of individuals that inhabit a specific geographic area and usually mate only with individuals within that limited area. A species with many scattered and abundant populations is less vulnerable to extinction than one that has only a few small isolated populations.

It is vital that we understand populations affected by human activities or the results can be disastrous. For example, an oil spill has the potential to kill thousands of sea otters. Such an impact would be disastrous to the California population of about 2,000 otters, but less destructive to the Alaska population, which numbers over 200,000.

How Many Whales?

Whales and dolphins are spread over large areas of oceans, swim vast distances, and spend most of their lives under water, where we cannot see them. It would be impossible to try and count every individual! But scientists can estimate the total population of an area by counting only a small sample; they use two basic methods—line transect and mark/recapture.

The line transect method involves counting along a particular route for an estimate of the animals within a narrow area. For example, if you wanted to esti-  mate the number of people in a large park on a very foggy day, you could walk along several paths and count people as they appeared from the mist. You could tell

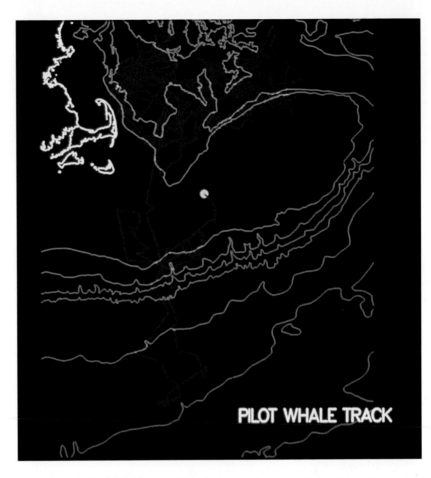

PILOT WHALE TRACK

how far you could see on either side of the path, and at the end of the walk you could calculate that you saw an area equal to about 10 percent of the park. If you saw eight people on your walk, and you know you covered 10 percent of the park, you could estimate that 80 people were in the park on that foggy day. (If 8 people equal 10 percent, then 80 people equal 100 percent.)

A line transect survey for cetaceans works like this walk through the park, except that the person counting is usually in a boat or an aircraft. And with cetaceans, an additional estimate has to be made of how many animals on the survey route were not counted because they were under water when the observer went by. In the case of the gray whale, the animals are the ones to go by, and the observer is stationary on the top of a cliff!

A computerized tag on a pilot whale feeding and diving off the coast of New England (yellow line) relayed information on its movements to scientists via satellite; this computer plot of its behavior (red line) is the result. COURTESY BRUCE MATE, OREGON STATE UNIVERSITY, HATFIELD MARINE SCIENCE CENTER.

LEFT:
The age of a whale can be determined by counting the layers of dentine or cementum on its teeth. This tooth from a Cuvier's beaked whale has 64 layers. USNM 259129; DICK MEIER.

For mark/recapture studies, a certain number of individuals within a population are marked or tagged so they can be easily spotted later. For example, if you wanted to know how many people were attending a very large party, where the guests were constantly moving around, you could first tag a small number of people—say, 20 guests—by placing red stickers on their backs. When you later look around, you find that one out of ten people, or 10 percent, have the red tags on their backs. You then know that your 20 tags represent 10 percent of the total population at this party and can estimate that the total population is 200 (1 out of 10 equals 10 percent; therefore, 20 people equal 10 percent, so 200 people equal 100 percent).

The mark/recapture method for studying cetaceans was first used in the 1920s by shooting small metal cylinders called Discovery Tags into the blubber layer of large whales. These tags were recovered, sometimes years later, after the whale was harpooned and the blubber removed from the carcass. Later, biologists attached various types of tags to dolphins for population studies. With the spread of the photo-identification technique, the natural markings of animals are now used as tags in counting populations, and the living animal can be sighted again and again!

Members of the Band: DNA

To learn more about cetaceans, researchers look to the grandeur of space when they use satellite tags and to the miniscule world of molecules when they analyze DNA.

DNA is the genetic "blueprint" for most living organisms and is found in virtually every cell in the body. Because DNA is abundant in skin cells, only a small tissue sample is needed for DNA analysis. It is easy to collect tissues from stranded animals, and small plugs of skin and blubber can be removed from free-swimming whales and dolphins using a biopsy dart.

The DNA is extracted from a tissue sample, processed, and blotted onto a special gel, where it forms a pattern of bands that can be analyzed. In one type of analysis, called sequencing, the scientist compares samples from various animals, looking at the particular bands that differ from one population to another. Studying these bands allows whale experts to identify populations of cetaceans and helps them to determine the evolutionary relationships among species.

Another DNA analysis technique, called DNA fingerprinting, focuses on the pattern of bands that is unique to each individual. DNA fingerprints are particularly helpful in identifying the close relatives—the parents and offspring and the sisters and brothers—within a pod of whales or dolphins.

TOP:

A scientist uses a biopsy dart to collect a plug of skin for DNA analysis from a right whale. SCOTT KRAUS, NEW ENGLAND AQUARIUM.

MIDDLE:

In the laboratory, sophisticated equipment is used to perform DNA analyses on tissues to determine if various individuals and populations are related. PATTY ROSEL.

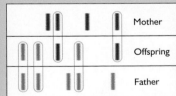

Mother

Offspring

Father

Simplified DNA profiles for three cetaceans. The DNA fingerprint of a cetacean calf includes some bands inherited from its mother and others from its father, and this feature can help scientists identify an unknown parent. If a DNA sample from the calf's mother is available, for example, they can separate out the bands that she contributed to her offspring's DNA profile so that it is easier to see the bands contributed by the father. By comparing the latter bands with those in the DNA fingerprints of all of the males likely to have sired the calf, its father can be identified. NATURAL HISTORY MUSEUM OF LOS ANGELES COUNTY, BIOSYSTEMATICS LABORATORY; JAMES COIRE ANGUS.

V CONSERVATION

uring the eighteenth and nineteenth centuries, when whaling was big business, a catch of a large whale was worth a small fortune. In fact, the oil of the right whale was so valuable that it was sometimes accepted as money. This species was known as the "right whale" to catch because of the volume of oil it yielded, the quality of its baleen, and the fact that, when dead, it floated. The right whale was the first species to be hunted almost to extinction by whalers. The slaughter of both mature and immature whales led to our concern today over how to protect and conserve them.

Overhunting is particularly dangerous to cetaceans because they mature slowly, and each produces only a few offspring in its lifetime. Populations of some whale species, such as the right whale, have been protected from hunting for over 50 years but only recently are showing any signs of recovery.

Modern Whaling

At the end of the nineteenth century, whaling became more and more mechanized. Whalers had earlier developed harpoons with exploding tips to kill the whale faster and guns to shoot the harpoons farther and faster. In 1868 these tools were combined by Svend Foyn, a Norwegian whaler; he created the harpoon gun, which was mounted on the front of a fast, motorized boat and used to stalk the largest of whales—the blues and finbacks and their kin.

In the early 1900s, commercial whaling was concentrated off Antarctica.

PAGES 84–85:
A modern whaling vessel returns to port with a catch of rorqual whales. MC TAGGART, GREENPEACE.

LEFT:
A whaling ship's gun. CAMPBELL PLOWDEN, GREENPEACE.

GOING, GOING . . . GONE?

Although no species of whale or dolphin has yet become extinct because of humans, the whole population of Altantic gray whales did disappear, probably because it was hunted to extinction. And many populations of large whales, such as the right whales, are only now beginning to recover from whaling and have dangerously few animals left. Unfortunately, two species of small cetaceans may become extinct within only a few decades: the baiji of the Yangtze river in China and the vaquita, found only in the northern Gulf of California.

The vaquita (Spanish for "little cow") is a small porpoise that was first described scientifically very recently, in 1958. Because it lives in such a small territory, it is very vulnerable to extinction. For years, it has been accidentally caught in nets set for a large fish called the totuava. Now both the vaquita and the totuava are in danger of becoming extinct because of overfishing. The Mexican government has banned people who fish from taking totuava, has passed laws to protect the vaquita, and has created a new sanctuary. But in this remote and sparsely populated region, it is difficult to enforce the ban, and illegal fishing continues.

A vaquita (at front) has accidentally been killed in a net set for fish.
FLIP NICKLIN, MINDEN PICTURES.

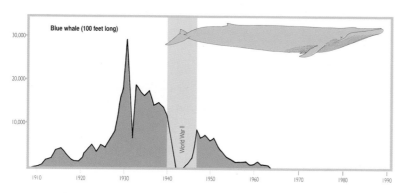

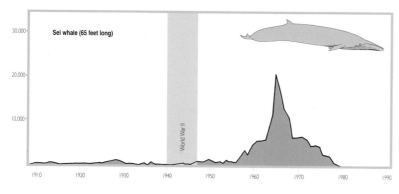

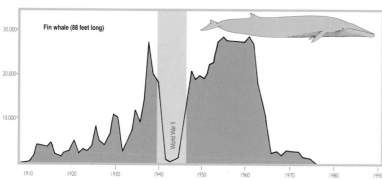

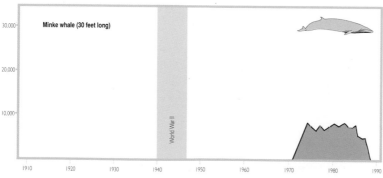

NUMBERS OF WHALES CAUGHT

Whale catches in Antarctica from 1910 to 1990. As the populations of one great whale declined, whalers began to hunt the next largest species. CYRENA NOUZILLE.

In these biologically rich waters, whalers from many nations relentlessly pursued rorqual whales. As each species became depleted, the next smaller species became the primary target. Species by species, populations of great whales were severely reduced: first the blue whale, then the finback, then the sei whale.

In 1946, most of the whaling nations agreed to regulate their whaling efforts and united to form the **International Whaling Commission**, or IWC. The primary goal of the IWC was to ensure that there would be enough whales for a healthy whaling industry. Early attempts to regulate whaling were not intended to save whales from extinction, but were primarily meant to prevent a glut of whale oil on the market, which would drive down the oil's value.

For the first three decades of its existence, the IWC did little to conserve whale populations. In the early 1970s, however, there was a shift in the IWC position. People in many western countries became opposed to whaling, and more member nations of the IWC reflected this public position.

In 1986, the IWC voted to suspend all commercial whaling until some future time, specifying that the consent of two-thirds of the member nations would be required to repeal the moratorium. Now the commercial whaling industry, once the gravest threat to the existence of many species of whales, has all but collapsed. Several countries, however, are trying to resume whaling now or in the near future.

Accidental Deaths in Fishing Gear

With whaling declining, conservationists have focused their attention on the plight of smaller cetaceans—the dolphins and porpoises and their cousins.

THE TUNA/DOLPHIN CONTROVERSY

In the late 1950s, people who fish for tuna stopped using fishing poles and switched to purse seines, long nets that are set in a large circle. Once the purse seine is set, the bottom is drawn together by ropes, forming a large bag with the fish caught inside. This bag is then slowly pulled onto the fishing boat, and the tuna in the net are collected and frozen.

For unknown reasons, schools of yellowfin tuna in the eastern tropical Pacific swim under large schools of dolphins, especially spinner, spotted, and common dolphins. People fishing are able to locate the tuna by searching for dolphins. But the purse seine nets catch both the tuna and the dolphins. Sadly, many dolphins have been drowned in the nets; in the early days of the purse seine fishery, over 100,000 dolphins died each year.

The U.S. Marine Mammal Protection Act of 1972 required that this enormous kill of dolphins be significantly reduced. By modifying their fishing gear and changing how they set the nets, people in the tuna industry had by the early 1990s reduced the kill to less than 10,000 animals. This was a tremendous decrease but was still too many dead dolphins in many people's opinion.

Public and political pressure was placed on the tuna industry to stop setting nets around schools of dolphins, and to instead harvest only "dolphin-safe tuna," which are fish caught without making use of cetaceans. Dolphin-safe tuna can be found, sometimes underneath floating objects such as logs. But they are often young and may not yet have had a chance to reproduce, and this in turn may lead to future problems with abundance of tuna populations. In addition, methods of fishing for dolphin-safe tuna sometimes result in large catches of many other species of fish, which are only thrown away. While the new method reduces the kill of dolphins, it may significantly damage the environment in which the dolphins live.

Unfortunately, there is no easy solution to the tuna/dolphin controversy. People in the tuna industry, scientists, and conservationists are still working to find a better way to feed people, preserve tuna, and protect dolphins.

A tuna boat's purse seine net (top), and an underwater view of pantropical spotted dolphins caught inside a net of this type. INTER-AMERICAN TROPICAL TUNA COMMISSION.

One of the biggest problems for these species today is their accidental capture in fishing gear, particularly **gill nets**. These widely used nets, which are set to hang vertically in the water, are usually made of monofilament (the same material used in fishing line) and are quite strong and almost invisible under water. Fish swimming along become entangled in the nets and are later recovered when the net is pulled in. Unfortunately, gill nets ensnare not only fish but also any other animal too big to swim through the nets' webbing. Large numbers of diving birds and marine mammals—cetaceans, seals, and sea lions—die in gill nets each year.

In 1992, the United Nations banned the use of gill nets, but hundreds of thousands are still in use. In the meantime, dolphins—once caught accidentally—are now deliberately being hunted: in Peru and Sri Lanka, almost 10,000 small cetaceans are killed every year to be sold as meat in the marketplace.

Pollution and Habitat Destruction

Humans living in coastal areas use the ocean as a place to dump most of their waste, including sewage and the thousands of chemicals used in home and industry. Until recently, the attitude towards ocean dumping was "out of sight, out of mind." As one result, some coastal dolphins have absorbed chemicals from our waste and have the highest levels of chemical contaminants in their tissues of any animals ever tested. Because cetaceans are so difficult to study, no one yet knows the effects of these chemicals. We do know, however, that some chemicals make other mammals more vulnerable to disease and reduce their ability to reproduce.

Habitat destruction is another

problem, and species that live only in limited areas are most susceptible to its effects. A dramatic case is that of the baiji, a freshwater dolphin that only lives in the Yangtze River in China. The baiji's river territory is in the most populated country in the world, where boat traffic, fishing, and damming have contributed to its endangerment. The government of China has taken many steps to protect the baiji, but it is difficult to change the activities of so many people along such a heavily used river. In the meantime, the government has set up protected areas where, hopefully, the baiji can find refuge.

Another possible pollutant is noise. Human activities in the ocean, such as oil exploration, ocean drilling, and shipping, produce loud noises. We do not know what effect such noises have on cetaceans, who rely heavily on sound and hearing to communicate, navigate, and find food.

The Role of Research

In planning for the conservation of marine mammals, many factors must be considered, including economics, cultural and ethical values, the biology of the animals, and even the ocean ecosys-

OPPOSITE:
A dolphin swims near a fishing net. Many cetaceans and diving birds are accidentally killed in nets designed to catch fish.
HOWARD HALL/HOWARD HALL PRODUCTIONS.

The baiji, which is only found in China's Yangtze River, may become extinct because of human activities in its habitat, in spite of a Chinese government conservation program designed to save it.
BERND WÜRSIG.

tem itself. If gill nets can no longer be used, for example, people who fish for a living must buy different kinds of nets, possibly ones that require more workers; this could be expensive, and fish products in the market could become less available and more costly.

There is often very little money available for addressing conservation issues. Scientific research can provide the information needed to assess, for example, the impact of human activities on wild cetaceans. But hard decisions must still be made. It is possible to spend a tremendous amount of money and effort saving a few individuals of an abundant species while ignoring a more perilous situation that threatens an entire population.

In balancing our needs as people with the needs of other creatures we value and want to protect, we must have the best information that we can get. The work of scientists will continue to be vitally important in identifying conservation problems and suggesting possible solutions.

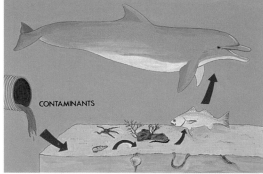

Cetaceans get trace pollutants into their tissues and organs by eating contaminated prey. Some coastal dolphins have the highest levels of chemical contaminants in their bodies of any animal yet studied; no one knows what effects these chemicals may have on the dolphins' lives. CYRENA NOUZILLE.

Dolphins offered in a fish market in Sri Lanka. FLIP NICKLIN, MINDEN PICTURES.

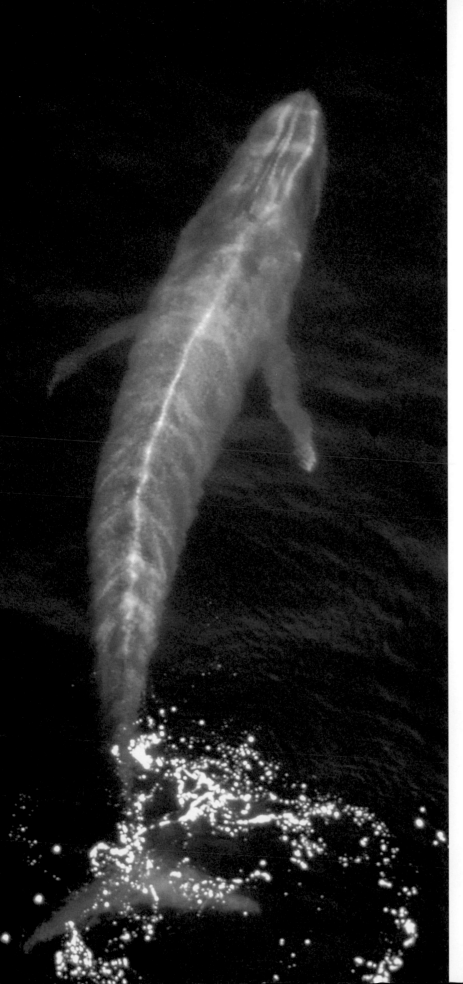

WHAT CAN YOU DO?

There are almost 6 billion humans on earth. If each one of us makes an effort to protect our planet, together we can have a great impact.

Recycle and Reuse. Recycling and reusing are two of the simplest ways you can help the environment. Anything that is recycled does not need to be dumped, and fewer raw materials must be used to replace it.

Use Less Energy. Every time you leave a light on or drive needlessly, you are wasting energy. Your conservation effort means that less oil must be transported, and fewer hydroelectric dams or other powerplants must be built.

Don't Dump Anything Into Storm Drains. Everything that goes into gutters and storm drains eventually ends up in the ocean. Take used motor oil or other chemicals to a proper disposal site.

Become Informed. The more you learn about conservation, the better able you are to minimize damage to the environment.

Become Active. Join one of the many conservation organizations. Take your time to pick one that represents your views and is effective. Write your government officials to let them know how you feel about an issue.

MICHELE HALL/HOWARD HALL PRODUCTIONS

LEFT:

Blue whales were hunted to near extinction during the twentieth century. FLIP NICKLIN, MINDEN PICTURES.

93

WHALES HEAD,   CAPTURED

LONG BEACH CAL, MAY 20TH 97,
C.J.D.   No 105

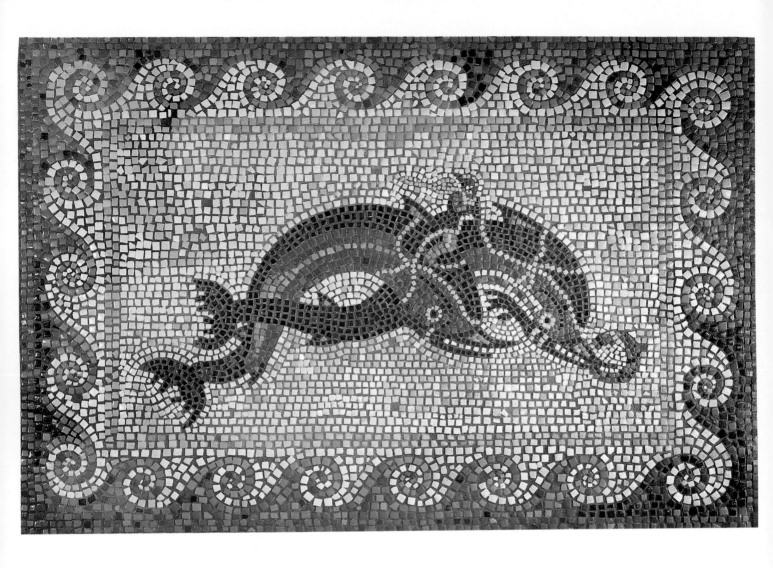

PAGES 94–95:

A fin whale that stranded at Long Beach, California, in 1897 attracted a crowd of local residents. LACM 54761, NATURAL HISTORY MUSEUM OF LOS ANGELES COUNTY, MAMMALOGY ARCHIVES.

ABOVE:

A replica of a mosaic in the House of Dolphins on Delos, the Greek island said to have been the birth place of Apollo. In an ancient Greek myth, Apollo takes the form of a school of dolphins and leads a lost ship to safety. REPLICA BY CAROL RYAN.

RIGHT:

Dolphins are depicted in ancient Greek tombs and on vases and coins. DICK MEIER.

From earliest times, people have encountered whales and dolphins in the sea or on its shores. Both ancient and contemporary cultures have incorporated the whale, as a source of meat and oil and as a symbol of grace, power, and mystery. Through science and art, we are still trying to know and learn from these ocean-going mammals.

Greek and Minoan Civilizations

As with many coastal cultures, the ancient Greeks depended on the ocean as a source of food. As a result, images of marine life—including whales and dolphins—were present in everyday Greek life.

Stories of dolphins befriending and saving people were especially common among the ancient Greeks. One of the most beautiful legends tells the story of Arion, the finest lyre player of his time. After earning a great deal of money, Arion took passage on a ship journeying to Corinth. When its sailors discovered Arion's wealth, they plotted against their passenger, planning to steal his money. Arion discovered the plot and begged for his life, but his pleas were

A PALACE FIT FOR A DOLPHIN

More than 4,000 years ago, the Minoan civilization thrived on Crete, an island off the southern coast of Greece. Minoan culture was famous for its elaborate palaces and beautiful art work.

The Minoan fresco from the Queen's Room at the Palace of Minos at Knossos represents Minoan talent—it is richly decorated with images of dolphins. This cetacean fresco survives even today despite two earthquakes that destroyed the Palace itself, the first in about 1700 B.C., and the second in about 1400 B.C. The dolphin wall remains as testimony to this rich culture and its interest in cetaceans.

Minoan depictions of dolphins are relatively true to life. In contrast, medieval drawings of dolphins made many centuries later show them as fish-like creatures with gills and scales. REPLICA BY CYRENA NOUZILLE.

ignored: he was ordered to take his own life or have it taken from him. Arion persuaded the crew to allow him to sing one last song, then he bravely threw himself over the side of the ship.

Unseen by the crew, a dolphin appeared; it saved Arion and took him to shore, where he recounted the treachery of the crew. Later, when the sailors landed, they were asked about their passenger. Because they were unaware of Arion's amazing rescue, the crew members falsely reported that the musician had been safely taken to his destination. When Arion stepped forward, the men realized they were trapped in their lies and admitted their guilt.

The Tlingit

Native peoples of the northwestern coast of North America incorporated whales into their cultures in different ways. Some ate whale meat and used the bones and other body parts for tools. Others painted and carved images of whales in their arts. Many cultures told stories. The Tlingit ("klin-kit") of southeastern Alaska had a tradition that was unique among Native Americans of the Pacific Northwest: Tlingits rarely hunted whales, but instead immortalized them in their beliefs and used their images on masks, blankets, housefronts, and totems.

Tlingit clans told and acted out stories about whales, and these stories have been passed down through the generations. One account is of the origin of the killer whale.

A man from the Seal people created killer whales. He tried to carve whales out of many different kinds of wood; first, red cedar, then hemlock, and then many other kinds. He then took his carvings to the beach and tried to make them swim, but each carved whale only floated. The last type of wood he tried

TOP:

The blankets that these Tlingit men wear incorporate images of killer whales. NEGATIVE 2A 134499, DEPARTMENT OF LIBRARY SERVICES, AMERICAN MUSEUM OF NATURAL HISTORY.

RIGHT:

A modern Tlingit wooden hat with a killer whale effigy, made by Carmen Plunket. JUSTIN DE LEON.

Killer whale images on the front of a Tlingit house.
ALASKA STATE MUSEUM.

was yellow cedar, and when he took this carving to the beach, the whale swam.

The Seal people man carved many whales out of this cedar and then made them swim up the inlet. He taught the whales what they should eat and where they should go. The man told the whales to hunt for seal, halibut, and other sea creatures whenever they went up to the heads of bays. But he also told them not to hurt any people. Instead, people may ask the whales to give them something to eat.

Before this man carved the yellow cedar, there were no killer whales.

The Tlingit believed that as a reward for not hunting them, killer whales would provide people with blessings, including food. Tlingit sometimes threw their children into the waves of a killer whale passing near the beach, asking the whale to ensure the strength and health of their children.

Nineteenth-century New England

In the 1700s and 1800s, New Englanders relied on whaling to support their economy. They quickly depleted the local population of right whales and soon focused attention on the sperm whale.

The sperm whale produced a valuable oil, called **spermaceti**, in an organ

The Whale as Art

Whalers did not spend all their time at sea catching whales. There were long, boring days without any entertainment. Some idle sailors became artists using the only materials they had—whale teeth, bone, and baleen. The art of **scrimshaw** was born.

Scrimshaw was usually made from the teeth of a sperm whales. One surface of the tooth was polished smooth, often using shark skin as sandpaper. An image was etched into the smooth surface with a needle; to make the design stand out, lamp soot, called lampblack, was then rubbed into the etched tooth.

Whalers also made teeth, bone, and baleen into household items, including checkerboards, dominos, knitting needles, rolling pins, rings, bracelets, and salt shakers. The men often made presents of the scrimshaw and carvings for their wives or girlfriends back home, proof of how homesick they were.

DICK MEIER

in its head. Spermaceti was used to produce candles that were smokeless, a desirable feature at a time when homes were lit only by candles. Additionally, the gut of a sperm whale sometimes contained a mysterious substance called **ambergris,** which could be used to make cosmetics, love potions, headache remedies, wine flavoring, and, most importantly, perfume.

In the mid- to late 1800s, demand for the baleen of the right and bowhead whales surpassed the market for oil of the sperm whales. The baleen from bowhead and right whales is quite long and could be cut, boiled, and shaped easily. When dried, it retained the shape it had been given and yet was flexible, having the qualities of today's plastic and spring steel. Baleen was used for tongue depressors, the stays of umbrellas, and buggy whips. During the 1860s, the style of a woman's dress called for a small waist, and corsets and hoops of whalebone were used to cinch the waist and create a full bodice and skirt. Baleen was also used as switches to spank naughty children, which is where we get the expression "to give someone a whaling."

In time, Yankee whalers had to travel greater distances to respond to the growing demand for baleen and oil, going all the way to the Arctic Ocean to search for whales. Soon bowhead whaling, like the right whale industry, collapsed because of over-exploitation. With the discovery of petroleum and the growth of the spring steel industry, whale products were replaced and, during the early 1900s, Yankee whaling declined.

The Eskimo

More than 1,000 years ago, coastal Eskimos began to depend heavily on marine mammals to support them in the harsh polar climate. They used whale products themselves and also

traded them with inland tribes for wood, caribou skins, and other resources.

The Eskimos of the northern coast of Alaska hunted both bowhead and gray whales, which migrate into Arctic waters during the summer. Every part of a whale's body was consumed or frozen for future use. The Eskimos ate meat, intestine, and blubber, and they used blubber for fuel, whale bone for house supports, and baleen for fishing and hunting tools. The whale hunt was one of the most important events in coastal Eskimo society.

Various ceremonies accompany the hunt. Eskimos believe that the whale allows itself to be killed and that its skull must be returned to the ocean to guarantee that its soul will be immortal

ABOVE:
An artist's view of a hunt for gray whales in the lagoons of Baja California in the mid-1800s.
FROM *THE MARINE MAMMALS OF THE NORTHWESTERN COAST OF NORTH AMERICA . . . .,* BY C. M. SCAMMON, 1874 (REPRINTED BY DOVER, 1968).

LEFT:
Sperm whale alongside a whaling boat, circa 1900.
NEW BEDFORD WHALING MUSEUM.

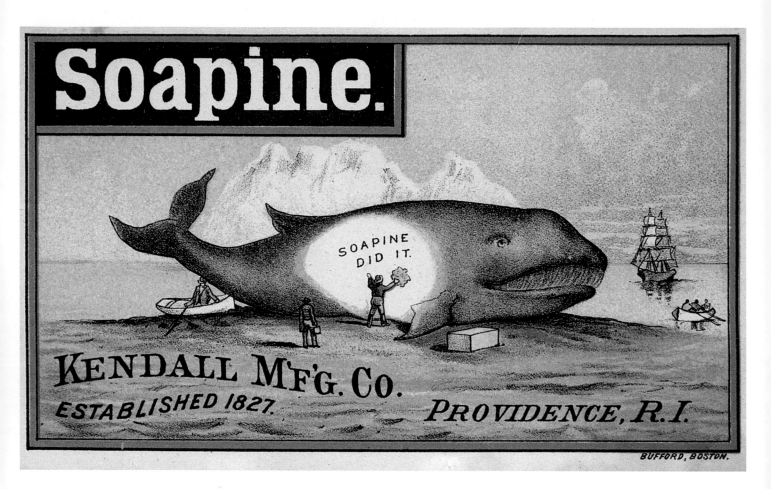

and its body will be reincarnated. In their tool kits, Eskimos keep various amulets, or good-luck charms, to use in hunting rituals. The seal-skin floats on their harpoons are often decorated with the face of a person or animal who, according to tradition, will lead the hunter to the whale.

The discovery of oil in Alaska affected Eskimo whaling practices. With the sale of their mineral rights to oil companies, many Eskimos previously unable to hunt whales could now afford the necessary boats, equipment, and crews. The number of hunters and the number of whales caught doubled immediately after the economic boom caused by the Alaska pipeline.

Currently, the International Whaling Commission permits the Eskimos of Alaska to hunt whales out of respect for their culture, which has been and still is tied to the whale. The Eskimos themselves formed the Alaska Eskimo Whaling Commission to study the situation: every few years the quota of whales killed is reassessed. Since 1978 the annual limit has grown from 14 to 41, an increase resulting from higher estimates of bowhead whale populations.

103

EPILOGUE

The history of people and whales contains stories that help explain the fascination people have always felt for cetaceans and our desire to sometimes invest them with remarkable powers. The more we learn about these masters of the ocean realm, the more we realize that they are remarkable as they are, without any help from us. The story of Pelorus Jack undoubtedly has elements of fantasy as well as truth and says as much about people as it does about dolphins.

In 1888, a dolphin appeared in a treacherous sea channel at the D'Urville Islands off New Zealand The crew of a ship called the *Brindle* first saw the dolphin bobbing up and down in front of the ship. To their amazement, the dolphin guided the ship through the dangerous channel to safety.

Known as Pelorus Jack, the dolphin continued to guide all ships through the channel for many years. But in 1912, a drunken passenger on board the *Penguin* shot Pelorus Jack, wounding him seriously. Weeks later, the dolphin reappeared and again began to guide ships. But whenever the *Penguin* showed up, the dolphin would swim away—he would not guide that ship. Without Pelorus Jack, the *Penguin* was eventually wrecked and sank in the same channel.

The truth is that Pelorus Jack, identified as a Risso's dolphin, did bowride steamers in the D'Urville Island region, but, according to some accounts, the dolphin refused to go into the straits. Although there is no official record of its having been shot by any passenger, it seems true that the dolphin did not like the *Penguin*. Pelorus Jack may have avoided this particular ship because it was noisy—it had two propellers instead of the usual one.

If there is a lesson in the Pelorus Jack myth and its embellishments, it is that none of us wants to be involved in activities that endanger the lives of whales and dolphins. The contemporary legend, true or exaggerated, carries a message for our modern times—the ways in which we behave toward the natural world may determine how well we ourselves survive.

A humpback whale starts a deep dive by throwing its massive flukes into the air. JOHN E. HEYNING.

lack teeth but possess baleen for filtering food out of the water and that have two blowholes.

Odontocete The suborder of cetaceans that possess teeth, have a single blowhole, and can echolocate.

Parasites Organisms that live on or in another organism and do not benefit the host.

Plankton Small plants and animals in the ocean that drift with the currents.

Pod A group of whales or dolphins.

Population, or **subspecies,** or **stock** A group of members of a species that rarely breed with members of other populations of the same species, often because of geographical separation.

Rorqual Baleen whales of the family Balaenopteridae that possess numerous throat grooves.

School A group of dolphins or porpoises.

Scuba The equipment, including tanks and regulators, that allows divers to carry a supply of air and to breathe underwater.

Sexual dimorphism The differences in size, shape, or color between the male and female of a species.

Shunting With blood, to shift the primary flow from one group of blood vessels to another group of blood vessels.

Species A group of organisms that can breed with each other.

Spyhopping A whale's behavior of sticking its head up out of the water.

Stock See **Population.**

Stranding The running aground or beaching of a cetacean, either alive or dead.

Subadults Animals that are no longer dependent on their mothers but are not yet fully mature adults.

Subspecies See **Population.**

Systematics The classification of organisms and the scientific study of the evolutionary relationships among them.

Modern families of cetaceans.

Family	Common Name	No. of Species	Comments
Balaenidae	Right whales, bowhead whale	3	Worldwide in temperate to tropical waters
Balaenopteridae	Rorqual whales	6	Whales with numerous throat grooves; includes blue and humpback whales
Eschrichtidae	Gray whale	1	Migrates along Pacific coast of North America
Neobalaenidae	Pygmy right whale	1	Smallest baleen whale, lives in Southern Hemisphere
Physeteridae	Sperm whales	3	Includes the largest of the toothed whales
Ziphiidae	Beaked whales	19	Little-known group of deep diving whales
Platanistidae	Ganges river dolphin	2	Fresh water dolphins that live in India and Pakistan
Iniidae	River dolphins	3	Found in Yangtze river of China and fresh and coastal waters of South America
Monodontidae	Beluga and narwhal	2	Arctic species
Phocoenidae	Porpoises	6	Small, with rounded heads; most species coastal; found worldwide except tropics
Delphinidae	Oceanic dolphins	33	Worldwide in oceans and some rivers; species include the familiar bottlenose dolphin and killer whale

INDEX

A bold number indicates that the subject is illustrated; text about the subject may also appear on the same page.

Project Director: Robin A. Simpson

Design and Typography: Dana Levy, Perpetua Press, Los Angeles

Editor: Pamela Stacey

Production Coordinator: Letitia Burns O'Connor, Perpetua Press

Design and Computer Assistance: Darlene Hamilton

Index: Celeste Newbrough, Academic Indexing Service, Berkeley